Praise for
An Accidental Pilgrim

Maria Caponi was not a hiker. She is a woman whose early years were defined by the surreal experience of toggling a life in politically fractious Argentina and life as a Physics and Astronomy PhD student in the United States. In mid-life, she enjoys "routine, rest and procrastination," and even thinks it "silly to work this hard," when she hikes around Southern California with a group of friends. Going against the very grain of herself, she agrees to walk 220 miles of the 'El Camino de Santiago de Compostela.' The result is this enchanting story, of walking and bonding, overcoming grief and spiritual awakening. A life of journeys and adventures recounted in prose and poetry, with occasional visual snacks along the way.

Elizabeth Cohen,
poet and author of *The Family on Beartown Road*

AN ACCIDENTAL PILGRIM

*a memoir
in prose and verse*

Maria Z. Caponi

atmosphere press

Table of Contents

Dedication or Explanation

This is a hybrid memoir of a journey, or maybe of many journeys, and, as with any work of narrative nonfiction, it is part real, part imagination, and part exaggeration. It is also an elegy to my best friend of fifty years, my husband, Enrique, and an offering to the ghosts lurking in the back of my mind, an attempt to appease my guilt at being here while many others I loved are not. This is a journey that began decades ago, just after or maybe before I was born, and I expect that it will end, or maybe not, when I can no longer make a wish for a place to go.

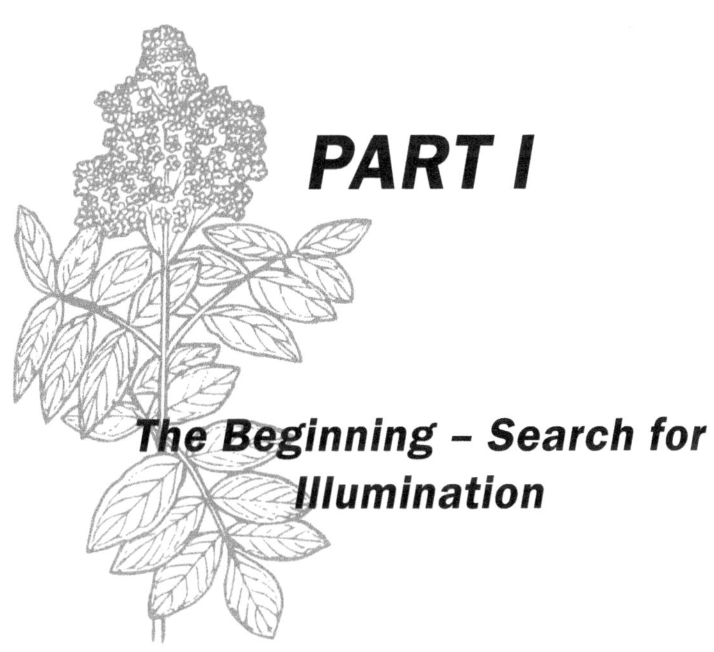

PART I

The Beginning – Search for Illumination

El Camino

A journey starts when we say it does and it ends when we realize we are no longer there. I am an atheist, secular, areligious Jew. So why did I embark on an arduous 200-plus-mile Christian pilgrimage hike with three Catholic women friends?

Intention

I walk and hear inside my head:
caminante no hay camino,
se hace camino al andar...[1]

I translate
for the friends
who will walk with me
part of the way:

Wayfarer, walker,
there is no path,
you make the path as you go.

We're all voyagers, wanderers,
traveling in time,
a journey unknown,
until we make it up.

But, my friends, they
still don't understand.

---

1. These are two lines from *Proverbios y cantares XXIX* by A. Machado

This was 1968

January 1968

The first time I left Buenos Aires, Argentina, where I grew up, it was January 1968. I was just 19 years old, single, so smart that it hurt, a trait I felt I had to hide. When I was 12 years old, I wanted to look grown up. I was riding in a car with my older cousin, who was four years older than I, and three of her friends. The friends were all boys and the one who was driving proposed a puzzle. One about a farmer crossing a river with a boat that can only carry two things at a time, but he has a goat, a wolf, and cabbage to move to the other side. Nobody could come up with an answer about how the farmer could manage to cross without losing the goat or the cabbage. "It is impossible," my cousin said. "I don't think it has a solution," one of the boys said. There was a silence, and in the quiet I blurted, "It is obvious." I could see it so clearly in my head and told them how it could be done. They all laughed, called me a nerdy brain. I felt embarrassed. It hurt, it was not cool to show that I could be bright.

I thought the move to the U.S. would be temporary, just for one year. A lie to myself. My father bought me a round-trip ticket good for one year and booked a one month return ticket for himself. "It will be like a long vacation," I said. One year later, in the U.S., my college boyfriend, Enrique, whom I had met in Argentina, became my husband. It took another seven years for both of us to return to Argentina — "Back home forever," we said, and then we left again.

The first time I left, I left behind almost everything I knew and loved. My home, my father, my family, my friends. But most of all, the long hours of passionate chats or tête-à-têtes over a tiny cup, a demi-tasse of strong, dark coffee at one of my neighborhood corner cafés.

I would miss those moments when we sat in groups of five or six, crowded around the small round marble tables that should have seated only three. We bumped elbows, our hands moving up and down and sideways to make a point, interrupting each other as we shouted our truths.

Moments like that day when Germán, after swallowing the last drop from his double espresso, yelled: "Our military, they are in the pocket of the Americans." The waiter, who was nearby, turned to look at him, raised his eyebrows and put a finger to his lips, a secret shush. Germán, his cigarette dangling from his half open mouth, ashes strewn all over his gray patterned sport coat, let out a snigger. I was tense — who knew who around us was listening to our rants? It was early July 1966. In June the Argentine military had overthrown the democratically elected government. There was talk that they planned to revoke academic freedom, the University autonomy that had been in effect since the university reform of 1918.

The first time I left, I left behind the fear. That day in the café I was nervous, but I was also excited, my face hot. I tried to get a word in but failed. I didn't know how to project my voice. I also think now that my opinions were not yet well formed. I had passion but no depth. Next to me, Pablo, a skinny guy who wore, winter or summer, a roll-neck black sweater, was eating all the peanuts at the table. He kept his voice down when he said, "The American imperialists invaded the Dominican Republic." But Germán was undeterred. He signaled for another espresso and yelled again: "The military are a piece of shit, they are going to end the University autonomy, we have to act!"

I looked toward the door of the café for the blonde guy I had been going out with for about half a year. He had a more analytical mind and a low inclination to scream, but he hadn't arrived yet. We went out most of the time as a group. The word 'dating' didn't exist at that time and in that place, we mainly 'went out with' someone.

Germán's voice rose a notch. I fixated instead on the glass of plain water, smaller than a juice glass, and the espresso cup and saucer the waiter set on the table for Germán. This time the little cup was half filled. It was a single, not a double espresso. The cup was smaller than his hand. His fingers were too big for the little handle, he clutched the whole cup in his palm. The cup was porcelain, the color of mayonnaise. It had wide smooth ridges all around and the top border was decorated with a thin gold guard. The saucer had a piece of chocolate next to the cup. I wanted to steal the sweet, I had already eaten mine. It was what I most loved when they served my coffee, the mini-sweet that came with it. Germán's cup had a crack on the rim. For a moment I thought that he would cut his lip and stop talking, but he didn't. I drank from my own glass of water.

The first time I left, I left behind the air that smelled like pastries, espresso, and nicotine, thick with clouds of cigarette smoke. The saucers brimmed with filtered and unfiltered stubs. Our bodies full of adrenaline, we thought we could solve all the problems of the world. I left behind the well-known streets with the movie houses, vinyl record stores and used bookstores, the blooming purple jacarandas in spring. A way of life that I cherished, but that I had also scorned many times. Because it was a way of life that, I believed, limited my freedom, didn't allow me to open my wings, and I needed to fly.

Thus, the first time I left, I was excited but not sad. I had been on a plane before, but never flown further than Uruguay, or Brazil, just a few hours away. This time I was going further. I would be traveling 5,200 miles away from home to North America, Imperialist America, and I didn't mind. The Argentinian military might be funded by the Americans, but I liked American movies. Inside my head I carried a passion for justice and independence, but I also carried the image of Doris Day singing in technicolor, a smile with perfect white teeth, her eyes crinkling with glee. In one part of my brain, I wanted to be her.

The last few weeks before my departure, I'd dreamed about water, oceans, lakes, even swimming pools. My father hid his tears, but I could see the glistening in his eyes, and sometimes at night, when he thought I wasn't looking, two drops would slide down his cheeks. When I noticed, he said that the TV hurt his eyes. I turned it off.

Still, I was excited but not sad. That trip was my future, we both knew.

The first time I left, it had been less than two years since the night of the long sticks. That night, at the end of July 1966, the military had finally stormed and occupied the University. This happened less than a month after that day in the café when Germán said the military would put a stop to the University autonomy. It was a night when the many students and professors who had remained inside the School of Science were arrested. The police struck all of them on the head with their batons as they came out of the building. Afterwards, almost all the professors resigned, and my world turned on itself. I was in my last year of college, and most classes had to be canceled. The University, that building I loved, no longer made me feel welcome.

Unclear on the concept of what it meant to depart my country, I was desperate to leave, and I left. One year after the revolution, the takeover, the military coup, most of us, the senior students without professors, wrote letters to apply to study abroad and my best friend translated and typed them, and all the ex-professors gave us references.

I was surprised when our letters got replies, with acceptances. We screamed the names of the universities, the logos on the letters that had accepted us: MIT, Brandeis, Harvard, Carnegie Mellon, John Hopkins, Maryland, Berkeley.

But I, I was unclear on the concept of what it meant to leave my widowed father alone, and my home, to go so far away. For me it was just an adventure. A chance to get away from the pressure to conform I felt around my family, my father's friends, even my own friends. In any case, I reassured myself, it would be just a short time away from home, an internship, I thought. My father would do fine. I would write him letters every day. I was young and naïve, of course.

Thus, that first time I left, I was excited but not sad. I was a follower, this would be a great ride, I was sure that in a year I'd be back. In January 1968, I boarded a flight from Buenos Aires to New York with my father. We would stay there for a week then fly to DC where I was going to attend the University. I was only 19 years old. He carried names and addresses of friends of friends, people who could help me when I'd be left alone, when he had to fly back home, also alone.

We carried two large, very large suitcases, molded gray plastic. Thick, substantial, heavy, with no wheels. The type you can no longer find, not even in garage sales. They carried my dresses, my jackets, my suits, my winter green Gamulán, the wondrous, heavy sheepskin jacket, a gift from my rich uncle, for good luck. There was a little space left for my father's clothes, but, after all, he would only stay one month. The bags were weighted with my notepads, as many books as I could fit, and my hope.

I was excited, but I was not sad. I believed that when we got there, to the promised land of the movies, I would be free. And then the plane landed. Our first stop: New York, Kennedy airport. I felt the cold. The cold of weather that I had never felt before. The cold on my bare legs, because in Buenos Aires in January it was hot, sweltering, and I didn't think to wear stockings. The cold in the language that I had thought I knew, but I didn't. The cold from the unfamiliar stares when I spoke.

Two weeks later, my classes at the University of Maryland began. I had to go to class. I was almost surprised to discover

Dad and I wearing my Gamulan, College Park 1968

that it was not an internship. I was enrolled in a PhD program. This was work, not a ride. I guess I hadn't paid enough attention to what we were applying for. I was happy to follow the lead of Enrique, my best friend, my boyfriend.

After a month, I found a place to live, a roommate. When my father left, I was settled in an apartment. I learned how to get to my classes and I was, for the first time in my life, on my own. I was a single, very young woman, working my way through graduate school in physics. For the first time, I felt invisible, or too visible. It depended. My words were not heard, except by my two friends from home, but my body was watched as cattle ready for the market, or a piece of meat, is watched. I ignored the stares, I focused on the work ahead, I denied the pain — after all, I had been doing that since my mother died when I was ten.

I sat at the large square wooden tables, in coffee shops that smelled of burgers and milkshakes. The waiter would bring a large glass of water filled with ice cubes and a straw before I could even ask for a cup of coffee. Then, the server would bring a brown-colored liquid in a large mug. The liquid was almost transparent, tasteless and weak. A distant cousin of the coffee I used to drink in Buenos Aires, and although there was plenty of sugar on the table, there was never a sweet, a candy, a piece of chocolate next to the cup. I always checked to see if the top of the mug had a crack.

I no longer felt excited. I was somewhat depressed, if not sad, when I figured I had to stay in the U.S. at least four more years, if not five, to finish what I had started. To get my graduate degree. I didn't know yet that it would be eight, in the end, before together with my husband I would go back home. By then, my father would be dead, most of my friends scattered around the world, and although we still brewed our coffee strong and dark, we drank it in large coffee mugs. From this journey, there was no way back.

Before we start

Southern California, USA

February-April 2019

Palos Verdes trail after the rains

Decision – February 2019

Of the four of us, all over 55 years old, only one has hiked before. Our friendships are interrelated through work, the town we live in and our kids. Three of us started to walk together after we retired. My husband of forty-five years, who had been diagnosed with lung cancer ten years ago, became sicker and died about that time. The breakfast and the company became, for me, a welcome distraction and a motivation to wake up early.

I don't know how to use trekking poles or wear a backpack in such a way that it wouldn't hurt my shoulders during long hikes. I also never, ever, wanted to wear hiking boots again, after a failed attempt thirty years ago when friends had invited my husband and I to walk with them in the Rocky Mountains. It had snowed, so there was ice on the trails. We didn't have any gear for hiking in snow, let alone on ice, so our friends lent us their extra pairs of boots. They would have been fine footwear for experienced hikers, or just hikers. For us, city born and bred, they were stiff, unyielding contraptions. We slithered, slipped and slid, and only didn't fall or hurt ourselves by the sheer luck of the young.

But things change. If your friends, the ones you walk with every week on the Strand along the beach, say they will hike across Spain, they will do El Camino,[2] and ask if you would go with them? You don't say no, at least I don't. I waver, vacillate,

---

2. El Camino refers to "El Camino de Santiago" (from the Latin *Peregrinatio Compostellana*, "Pilgrimage of Compostela"). Known in English as the **Way of St. James**, it is a series of trails leading to the shrine of the apostle Saint James in the Cathedral of Santiago de Compostela in Galicia, northwestern Spain. It is believed that the apostle is buried there and many walk or hike the trails as a form of pilgrimage or hoping for a spiritual revelation.

equivocate, hesitate and wait. They might forget. After all, El Camino is a pilgrimage, and from the start to the end, when you do El Camino Frances (or The Way of St. James, for Americans), it is 830 kilometers, 515 miles (I checked) and it usually takes about 35 days at a 'normal' pace of 25 kilometers/day. I'm pretty sure they don't have the time to do the whole thing. They worry about leaving their husbands to fend for themselves. Nelly worries that she has a meeting and will have to be back at a certain date. Margaret and I are more flexible and want to go all the way to Finisterre, 'the end.' My friends discuss their schedules, they plan, maybe in two weeks they could walk half of the Camino. My friend Nelly has a friend who did it, she wants to do the same. "If her husband, who is not in such great shape, could do it, we can too," she says. "There are stories of people in their late 80s, maybe even 90s, who do it."

"They must do only the last two days," I say. I don't think it will happen, that they will decide to go. I don't want it to happen. I don't want to think about another trip, and a pilgrimage hike at that. I don't need to make a sacred journey to reflect on my life or get a deeper understanding of my beliefs. I'm planning to be at a literary conference in Mexico in February, and a writing workshop in Paris in June. I can experience spiritual enlightenment by improving my writing, or just growing vegetables in my garden. Why on earth would I ever want to do a pilgrim walk in northern Spain in May?

But I have this fear of being left out. I have a fear of missing out on something exciting, something that could bring me joy. I am curious. I like to travel and I'm always on the lookout for something that takes me away from the routine of life. I love my routines, but I need the adrenaline of change and challenges to feel alive. Maybe I also need to feel that I am not alone. So, when my friends say, "We're sending the deposit, three of us, let us know if you want to be the fourth, if you're in," I say yes. I know full well that although I have my doubts, if they go and I stay, I will never forgive myself.

Then I go on a shopping spree for hiking gear.

I'm a Pendulum

A Foucault pendulum,
I vacillate.
I swing from side to side
in a straight line
while under my feet,
the earth rotates.

I oscillate

between the effort,
the desire, the wish
to grow, to learn,
the challenge
I'll conquer next

and

the easy way,
just to be,
to age in place.
A rocking chair,
yarn to knit,
a book,
a slow walk by the beach.

I fluctuate,
dangle,
teeter,

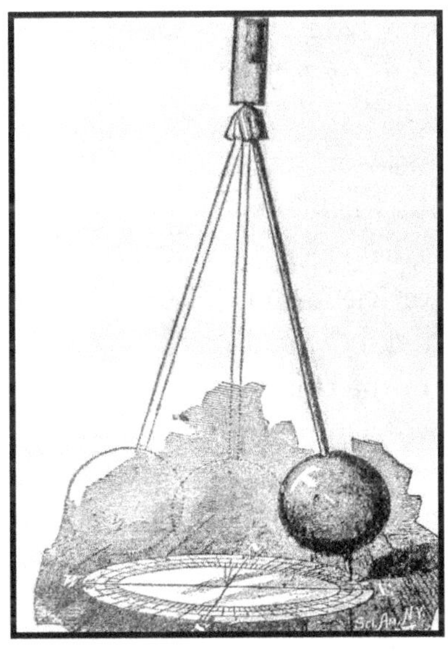

Foucault Pendulum Diagram
https://commons.wikimedia.org/w/
index.php?curid=61460948

pulled in one direction,
I swing back,
doubt,
between black and white,
then choose gray.

For every choice,
I see both sides,
take a long time,
never content.

I'm a pendulum,
that swings from anger
to many regrets.

Inside my core,
the weight.
A deep love
for friends now departed
and those still here,
for the smell of gardenias,
freesias, roses, sweet peas,
the rotten odor of boxwood.
For the tastes of chocolate,
coffee and wine,
for the nose licks of a dog,
and although I'm allergic,
the purr of a cat.
For life.

This love
doesn't swing,
never wavers,
stays.

Practice Hikes in Palos Verdes

Southern California, USA

March 2019

Palos Verdes map of one of the hiking trails (Portuguese Bend)
https://pvplc.org/_lands/docs/PBRBrochure2017.pdf

Hiking Equipment Test

Hiking equipment needs to be tested, they say. Thus, the experienced hiker, Nellie, the youngest of us at 57, led us on practice ascents and descents. "There are good trails around Palos Verdes, it will help us prepare," she said. I went along, although inside I thought: "This is probably a waste of time, if they are so sure that 90-year-olds have done the El Camino walk." I can be quite naïve sometimes.

Nellie lives in Palos Verdes, California, about 20 miles south of the rest of us, who live by the beach. If you could walk along the Pacific coast, following the turns of the ocean from our place to hers, you would see the landscape change from flat to hills, rugged cliffs where it becomes a hiker's paradise. But I'm not a hiker. As we plan these practice hikes, I question my sanity. Why am I doing this? And then, there is this surge of enthusiasm I always feel for what is new, different, a challenge. It is part of the duality of my personality. A type of schizophrenia of desires, a drive to confront, to dare the lazy part of myself.

We undertook our first hike in Palos Verdes, California. We hiked up on an area of sandy and rocky steep hills, after it had been raining non-stop for weeks. There was mud on all the trails. The sticky, sucking sludge stuck to our boots, to the bottoms of the poles and the legs of our hiking pants. We'd skid and slither before getting caught in the sludge. It was an effort to pull each foot up. It took two hours to hike less than two miles, then we gave up. Went for coffee and omelets at a nearby cafe. Three of us were sure that we would never find conditions like that along El Camino. The experienced hiker thought we were too soft, but she we wouldn't tell us that until later. For now she was kind with us newbies. If she pushed us too much it might backfire; we could get discouraged, or we might stop practicing.

The next two PV practice hikes were in dry terrain but on a steep trail, crammed with rolling rocks. It was hard going up; it was harder going down. Each one of us fell once. I believe I fell twice. Each time we lasted less than two hours, or two miles, before we gave up, congratulated ourselves, had a wondrous breakfast and patted ourselves on the back. The experienced hiker suffered in silence our lack of focus, our need to just have fun.

"Silly to work this hard," I said. "It will never be like this. I saw the pictures. It is a gravel path." Of course we could do this, every day, for two weeks, with just ten pounds on our backs. Then I thought about the pain I have every so often in my lower back. A sciatic nerve, they say. It comes and goes away. What if it stays when I have to hike so many miles with a backpack?

A Palos Verdes practice hike on a sunny day

Practice Hike
on the Strand

Southern California, USA

Early April 2019

Getting ready for a solo hike on the Manhattan Beach Strand

Practice Endurance

Endurance. I wasn't sure about that. We'd have to walk 12 to 15 miles every day for two weeks. I thought that could take more than eight hours on hard terrain. I wanted to know if I could last. None of the others worried about that, they were so sure we'd all be fine. After all, we had hiked for *two* full hours along the Palos Verdes cliffs. However, to check my stamina, I planned a dress rehearsal, just myself and the dog, who couldn't say no. We would start early, maybe at 8 a.m. to avoid the heat, and walk for six hours. That would be enough.

The night before, I readied my gear. The black hiking pants I'd bought at Target two weeks before. The ones that looked so ugly on the rack, I doubted I would ever wear them. They are supposed to not retain moisture and to dry quickly. Then, the top layers: a tank top that reads "My dog is my therapy," a wick-away-perspiration blue t-shirt, a light black sweater.

Next to the bedroom door I set the loaded new royal blue Osprey backpack. The one the adventure store attendant guaranteed would save my shoulders and my back. It is a contraption with a contoured mesh back frame and a zillion stays, a hip belt and harnesses — I've no idea what they are for, much less how to adjust them. Obviously, I've never been a backpacker.

I filled it with two one-liter bottles of water, rain pants, a rain jacket, some snacks, an emergency kit, some cosmetics, and even a scarf although today it's 70 degrees at the beach. After all, it is a *dress* rehearsal. I weighed it at 9.5 pounds and completed my costume with a dark green, floppy-brimmed sun hat and the Vasque boots with the thick socks that, the expert told me, would save my feet during long walks.

I didn't count on a backtalking brain or my laid-back, routine-loving self. I don't need much sleep, but I like to rest and procrastinate. "It's too early to get up," my mind said as soon as I woke up. "Did you check your emails, FB, Instagram, the weather?" The comforter was warm, and the doggy cuddled against my back. My brain kept going. "You forgot to add the vest. Are you sure it's enough weight?"

Two, or maybe three, hours later, I was all dressed up and ready to go. It was 11a.m. and before I left, leash in hand, I stopped by the door and took a selfie. I wanted to document this unusual play date with myself.

I walked 15 miles in all that day: the single block from my house to the park next to the wooden stairs, up to the top of the hill from where you can see the ocean, down the street to the beach and then along the Strand's concrete path to the end of Manhattan Beach, through Hermosa Beach and Redondo Beach. Each beach city has its own culture and landscape. Manhattan Beach has a family atmosphere, large houses that have become almost mansions in the last ten years. As you cross into Hermosa Beach there are more skateboards and bikes on the Strand, younger people milling around. The houses are smaller, although they are also beginning to build larger ones these days; as the older houses are sold and torn down, bigger dwellings go up. Redondo Beach is the largest of the three beach cities. There are many apartment houses and condos and a refinery at the end, the boundary where Redondo meets with the city of Torrance. There, by the refinery, I finally turned back. I could have kept walking, I told myself. I didn't have any pain, no sciatica acting up today, and I hoped it would stay that way. But I didn't want to get home too late. I don't like to walk on the Strand, or go up and down the stairs by myself, at night.

Gray Skies

It's a thing of beauty,
this gray sky.
A sorrowful and pregnant beauty.
In a moment,
it will pour its tears,
they will mix with mine.
In a moment,
the clouds will open up,
let out a ray of sunlight,
that will reflect from the ocean
to my eyes,
my lips will form a smile.

It's a thing of beauty,
all these hues of gray
the metal grays — silver, platinum, nickel —
the diffused grays — smoke, ash —
the violent grays — battleship, gunmetal —
or the dark grays — carbon, charcoal, jet.

It's a thing of beauty,
when the gray sky meets the ocean,
at the bluish gray
horizon line.
It gives birth
to the dark slate sea.

And there is beauty
in the spreading clouds,
the ridges on the wet sand,
the empty, wind-swept beach,
the rattle and clatter of the palm trees.
The pointed orange-green and red native grasses,
the cacti blooming with purple flowers,
and the yellow daffodils
under the gray sky,
opening.

Strand Walk

How did I endure 15 miles on the Strand? I stopped for brunch, coffee, an apple snack. Enough stops that I got back past 7 p.m. Less than six hours walking, more than two hours sitting down. I wasn't tired.

Easy, I told myself, *piece of cake. With enough coffee and stops, I can do this. I have been walking all my life.*

When I got home, I took off my boots, popped some popcorn, sat on the couch and fell asleep with the bowl on my lap and the remote in my hand. Then, I dreamed this:

I park my white Prius across the street from my house and watch a couple standing on my lawn. I think they are my gardener and his wife, but they look different. The woman is shorter and stockier; she wears a gray hoodie and the man, older than the one in real life, wears a cowboy hat. Both have long rifles in their hands, pointed towards the street, but there is nobody in the direction in which they point. I fret about my husband, who passed away four years ago. Is he still inside the house? (In my dreams, he's always alive, but rarely present.)

I hurry to the house next door, a dream-made-up one. In this vision, the house has a front patio and the neighbors are sitting around a table covered with a red vinyl tablecloth. It reminds me of a country house where we went on weekends, when I was a child in Argentina.

"You have to hide, there are scary people at my house," I say. I'm surprised — how can I act so calm?

A friend comes to visit the neighbor, and I tell him, "Stay, it's dangerous to be out."

I hear music and I know that there is a party at my house. Lots of people now. It annoys but doesn't frighten me. What would so many people do to my house? Is this an assault, an incursion, an invasion? Is my husband still in the house? Will he protect it from damage? I don't know what to do, so I go to sleep, on a cot, next to the patio, in my neighbor's house.

The next day is quiet. Everybody seems to be gone and I think: I've got to call the police, and my husband. Would the house be OK? I dial 411, not 911, because after all it is not an emergency. (This is a dream, there is no 411 for non-emergency police calls. 411 used to be what you dialed to find out someone else's phone number. They used to charge for those calls, and it annoyed my husband to no end when we used it instead of the free yellow book.)

An officer comes on the line and I explain. He says, "Call someone else, elevate. The police can't do anything." While we talk, I think about how long it would take me to get someone to look into this. I would rather call my husband to complain. He will know what to do. He would have protected the house. Is he OK?

I walk towards my house. I see on a window, a sign, it says: "Everything you want to do, you have already done."

When I woke up from the dream, I knew what this was. This was me, being calm and scared at the same time, up for a challenge but also hoping for what no longer is: my husband, who always had my back.

My husband died in his sleep, in our bed, lying next to me. I woke up in the middle of the night, or maybe I'd not been quite asleep, or maybe I had been awake since dusk listening to his elaborated breathing. I would wait for each change, his inhale my exhale, until I fell asleep. Until just at dawn when I touched his still chest, felt the void when I put my head next to his mouth. I didn't want to believe that he was not more, that the breathing I heard during the night had been his last. I kept thinking that it was just an interval, that he was sleeping, that he had found calm. And yet I knew. I had to start to learn how to live alone.

My younger son was at home. My friends came and sat shiva with us while we waited for my older son to arrive. I asked the funeral home to wait, to come later in the afternoon. I wanted to have one more day as if he were here alive. But the time came when two men arrived, wrapped him in a white sheet, and while I tried to kiss his cold cheek, held his hand, they took him away to be cremated. His wish, and mine.

Almost one month later, my older son and I went to pick up his ashes. They gave them to us in a green shopping bag, inside a cardboard box. The ashes white and fine like our beach sand, like his hair when he was young. We put most of the ashes inside plastic bags inside backpacks. A small portion, I separated and put into four lockets. One for each son, one for his sister, one for me. The next day we went up the stairs of our park, the same stairs my sons, Enrique and I had climbed together, puffing and huffing, so many times. We sprinkled some of the ashes from the plastic bags on the soil next to the stairs as we were going up.

So that day, a few weeks before our flight to start our Spain hike, I put around my neck the locket with the small amount of my husband's ashes inside. He would be with me when I got to Finisterre, "the end of the earth." The last stop, the 0 kilometers, after we'd crossed 200 miles of Spain.

Twisted Bark

I see you.
On my daily walk, ascending
the hill, 200 steps.

A piece of twisted bark,
by the side of the old
wooden stairs. A gray, brittle odd
shaped husk, looks like the back
of two legs, chest and head buried
in the soil, where we sprinkled
your ashes, white fine dust.

Where you and I
stepped together
Thanksgiving, that last time,
our sons and I, scattered you.
So much white powder. An urn full
dispersed under the canopy of
deep rooted ancient trees.

LAX, USA, to Chamartin, Spain

April 27-28, 2019

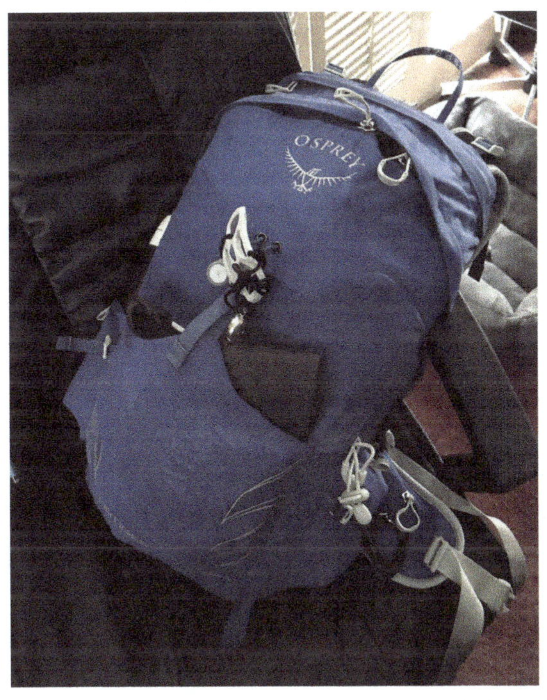

I am ready.

We Begin

We fly from Los Angeles to Madrid, the four of us, women who share the first initial of our names in pairs. The N's and the M's: Nellie, Nelly, Margaret and Maria in order of birth, from youngest to oldest – meaning me, Maria. We travel from LAX in pairs, at similar but different times. We M's have chosen a direct flight. The N's have chosen a flight with a stop-over in order to be able to shop at Heathrow on the way back. Sometimes we share interests in pairs, others we mix and match. And sometimes I'm the outsider, apart, disconnected from any combination of we four.

At the Los Angeles airport, after checking the bags and going through security, we meet in front of a duty-free store en route to our gates. We show off to each other the bursting backpacks we carry on our shoulders. Last week, the two N's found a sale and discarded the backpacks they had planned to use, acquired new ones, feeling immune to the potential risk of hiking with untested stuff. Nellie's is brown, large and seems comfortable on her shoulders. She is the experienced hiker, tall and strong. Nelly's is a bright yellow, a similar but larger model than ours, the M's. Nelly is exultant about hers; she likes orange, red and yellow hues. "I also got the bladder," she says, and we can feel her joy in the new toy, even though she still needs to learn how to use it. Three of us learned not too long ago the term "bladder": the hydration system built inside the backpack and containing a reservoir, or bladder, with a narrow hose that allows the wearer to drink hands-free.

Both N's love to shop. Nellie and Margaret also carry bladders. I refuse to deal with one. I carry a large water bottle in one of the backpack pockets, and a smaller one on a ring attached to the other side. We, the M's, carry the intense royal blue backpacks that we tested during our trial hikes. Three of us wear our Vasque hiking boots. Nelly carries hers inside her backpack. She likes fashion, to dress up, wears a black skirt, a handbag, a colorful scarf, and flip flops.

We're all excited to start this adventure and we compare our packing techniques, the weight of the bags we have just checked in. This is a self-guided journey, but with creature comforts, that Margaret and I have dubbed "glamo-hike." We'll carry our own backpacks, but our other bags will be transported from hotel to hotel as we walk. There are limitations and some cons to this arrangement, as we'll soon learn, as we walk from town to town. They will transport only one bag per person, with a weight of less than 35 pounds, and we have to make it to the next hotel, or we won't have a bag. And we have all packed too much.

I packed my usual carry-on with exactly 30 pounds of stuff, although I wanted to keep it to 25 pounds. With its four spinning wheels and practical handle it is light and easy to drag around, although I still have to check it at the airport. I can't carry it with me on the plane because it has the trekking poles inside. An unallowed item. The other three chose duffel bags. More space, but also more stuff and there is some worry that they weigh more than the allowed total. I mention that it might prove to be an effort to slog them around, carry them up and down stairs. "The trains, the hotels, everything has stairs in Europe, and seldom elevators to get the bags to your room," I say. "The transfer will leave them most of the time at the hotel lobby." "We can always pay for help," they say. Of course.

In pairs we part for our gates. We'll meet again tomorrow, the four of us, at the hotel by the Madrid Chamartin train station. After one night there, we will travel all together by train to Leon. Our adrenaline is running high.

Portal

I wait for my boarding group
to be called.
I'm anxious, I'm calm.
As always, I wonder,
what will I find,
at the end of this line?

When I board a plane,
for the umpteenth time,
when I fly over the ocean,
and when I finally land,
in a different land,
once again,
what will I find?

I don't know the name
or the shape or even the color
of what I search for.
I just know
I want to find
— when all I wish
is to stay and cry—
that place inside myself
that makes me dance.

Dreams and Tourism

On the plane I sit next to two young men in their twenties and eavesdrop as they chat. I'm full of adrenaline. I had planned to read, watch movies and eat, but instead I'm lulled by my companions' voices and I fall asleep. I dream, an intense and anxious dream. My brain is working overtime to clear its connections, get the mind ready for the challenges ahead.

I'm doing calculations inside a house with Nick, one of my PhD advisors from forty or more years ago. I get up to go to the bathroom. When I come out, the bathroom door now opens onto a park. I need to go around, I tell myself, I have to get back to the house because Nick is waiting. But I can't get back, I walk several blocks and I don't recognize the names of the streets. I don't have a phone to call and say I'm lost. I walk and think of what I will say when I finally make it: that I got confused, that I'm geolocation dysfunctional. Then, I see a young man. He is maybe 16 years old and I ask him where Montevideo street is. That's the name of a cross street near where I lived when I was a teenager. He says, "It's far, but you can go this way, it's at the end of this path." The path is a dirt track where people walk for exercise. It curves and goes on for a while and the young guy runs behind me to make sure I get to the end. I walk fast and pass a house where there is a man in a yard using a spray gun. I ask what he is doing. "Spraying DDT," he says. I hope he is kidding. Then, I hear someone saying my name. It is N.K. calling to me from a block away. He is with some other people and they are going to a party inside a sporting goods store.

"I found you just in time," he says, "I was about to give up." I mumble something about getting lost. I'm sweaty and feel out of place with that crowd. I'm twenty-years-old and I'm back in Argentina, and I wake up.

Wow, I tell myself, a whole memoir in a single dream, on a plane. That should take care of all the misgivings, the doubts that I have been hiding from myself. The plane lands and we are in Madrid.

Chamartin to Leon, Spain

April 28-29, 2019

Crab salad at Charmatin

Sunday Lunch

We arrive at Barajas, the Madrid airport, on a Sunday. Margaret and I go by taxi to our hotel in Chamartin, an administrative district of Madrid. We chose this hotel because it is next to the Chamartin train station. Tomorrow we plan to board a train at this station to go to the city where we'll start our pilgrimage-hike: Leon, Spain.

The ride to Chamartin from the airport takes less than fifteen minutes. Because this is a suburb, next to the station, and the hotel is hidden in a kind of alley, and it has a different name than the hotel name in our reservation, we doubt. I discuss in Spanish with the driver. The driver says, "This is the address… I think they changed the name." Margaret worries, "How come we didn't get a notice?" she says. But the driver is right, this is the hotel. Of course, I remember, it's part of the culture, the same as mine. The Spaniards are more relaxed than Americans about almost everything — alerts, rules, spending time at the table, being late to a meeting. A culture my walking friends will have to learn.

Because it is Sunday, all stores and restaurants are closed, but we find a bar next to the hotel that serves some cold stuff and beer. We sit at an outside table and order a crab salad, pretty much the only thing, besides bread and olives, that the restaurant has left to eat on a Sunday afternoon. And while we sit, we eavesdrop on the chats and belly laughs of a group of Spanish men at the next table. I translate for Margaret and we both suppress grins and giggles. Then we get a text message that the N's have arrived at the hotel. They have problems.

They couldn't sleep on the plane; they are exhausted and

there is a mix up: Nelly's reservation has not been paid. We text back. Don't worry, it will be sorted out. But Nelly just wants to go to her room and rest. Nellie checks in and comes out to find us at the table and sits with us for a few minutes, eats some crab salad, which she doesn't like, and then gets up to go back to the hotel. We M's tell Nellie to tell Nelly we will try to help her with the room mistake later, when we get back to the hotel. Now we just want to enjoy the rest of the day, the olives, the beer and the Spanish men laughing loudly next to us.

When we finally get back, we learn that Nelly was too anxious and she decided to just pay for the room. She texts Margaret, who had made the reservations, that she should pay her back. It is up to me to discuss with the front office, in Spanish, what happened. Margaret had paid for all of our rooms when she made the reservations, a while back. The woman clerk is relaxed and nice, she shows me the documentation, only three rooms were paid. She can't do anything about it and worries because Nelly was so upset. Margaret, who made the hotel reservations, says she will figure out what happened with the payment. In the meantime, she reimburses Nelly. Peace has been re-established.

We Take the Train

The next morning, after we all have all slept, we all seem fine and ready for adventure. After breakfast, we walk a couple of blocks to the train station. We lug our bags, three unwieldy colorful duffel bags and a black rolling carry-on, mine, up a long set of stairs and down to the gate. On our shoulders, the bursting backpacks. While we wait for the train, we ask a passerby to take a group picture of us. We are all so different and still, so alike.

A year later, I'll look at the picture and remember the moment, but by then I'll have a different perspective. Memories are not static, although I think pictures are. I said we had all slept, but in the picture we all look a bit tired, except maybe for Nelly. I check our faces, our postures. There is Nellie, a big smile on her face, relaxed, an orange sweater, her eyeglasses up. She leans on Margaret, who is anxiously happy, she holds her body tight but has let go of her backpack. Nelly and I have ours on our backs. My eyes are sleepy, I'm not wearing any makeup, I seem ready to go back to bed, but I'm happy, my mouth is also open with a big smile. And there is Nelly's big royal blue duffle bag, next to my small black carry-on. You can't see it in the picture, but all of us have Fitbits on our wrists. We are data-driven gals.

Does the picture show who we are? Does it show who leans on who, who is in the middle, who is on the outside? All of us are engineers or good at math, but one of us just lost her sister, and another's brother had a heart attack. Then another just had all her floors redone, she stays on task. And the fourth of us, that is me, she grieves for her lost partner while in her head, she writes.

At Chamartin Station, waiting for the train to Leon.

Arrival at Leon

Two hours later, when we arrive at Leon, I shine. I don't worry about transport, even if the hotel is several blocks away, I just walk. My companions lift and carry their heavy duffel bags, the little wheels of two of them are not so good on the cobblestone streets while I can roll with ease my carry-on. We cross unfamiliar streets and I check the Google map on my iPhone to look for the hotel. The people, the traffic, the signs in Spanish, the loud noise of a city in motion at noon, all steer my memories towards home. At the same time, I experience the well-known happiness of new possibilities.

I say, "This is what I like." To stride, to tread, to step, to pace, to amble, to march through the unknown streets of an old city and to get my iPhone up, click, click, a piece of the town inside. I don't think the others like this walking all that much. But they continue, nobody wants to be left behind.

How I Travel

You travel light, he said,
the passerby on my way,
as I walked, carry-on in hand,
the streets of Paris,
or Firenze,
maybe San Miguel de Allende in Mexico,
or somewhere in Jerusalem,
or perhaps Spain.
I forget.
I travel heavy, I said
I carry a shadow on my arm,
a chip on my shoulder:
the guilt of being here,
while others are gone.
I carry some confidence, lots of courage,
and all the memories stored inside my head.

It's hard to lift what I carry.
All the images, the sounds.
The smells and tastes of other trips,
of other walks,
of the same places,
or similar, now different.

While I travel, to lighten my load,
I make up stories in my head
and rush, bounce and prance,
on the gray cobblestone steps.

I travel with joy and anxiety.
I watch people walk,
in couples, with dogs, alone,
eyes fixed ahead,
looking for a friend.

I exhilarate — is this a verb?
Or maybe I just elate,
rejoice, stimulate.
I sigh with relief,
I take pictures,
a memory of the wooden door pattern,
the striped red and green fabric,
the woman on the street,
cooking *churros*,
sometimes *anticuchos*,
empanadas?
maybe *crepes* —
in case I forget.
I tear up with sadness,
sometimes happiness.
And all the time,
I look ahead
to this journey
I have embarked upon,
not yet at its end.

We Set Off

Leon, Spain

April 30, 2019

El Camino de Santiago, Leon to Finisterre

An Encounter with Gaudi

Too early to check in at our hotel in Leon, we leave the heavy bags with the hotel front desk clerk — a nice guy who gives us three packets that contain the maps, hotels and other needed information for the walk. Like school children, we grab the envelopes and check the maps, the guides and the badges needed to identify each bag as it is transported between hotels. But also, like children, we get anxious when we find that one packet is missing. For a moment nobody wants to give up their precious packet, until we become adults again and figure out that we can share. I tell my friends not to worry, this is Spain, they are not always as efficient as Americans but we will get another packet later. In fact, after some back and forth over the phone with the tour company, the mistake is corrected and the missing package is delivered in the late afternoon.

While our rooms are being prepared, we walk the city, ready for lunch. It's noon, all the tourist landmarks we want to visit are closed until 4 p.m., but not the cafés and the restaurants. I think that sitting at a table outside, in this old city, and watching the world go by, would be my idea of paradise. There is some discussion about where to go. What kind of food? Is it safe? I tell them, "Don't worry, Spanish food is delicious, doesn't matter where!" I know that is not quite true, but I also know that otherwise we'll be walking in circles until we're starving and we'll end up eating anyway, anywhere along the way. "This is a good place," I say with confidence, and encourage my companions to sit outside at one of the many restaurants lining an alley near the hotel. I have no idea if the food here will be any good, but I assume it's OK because the place is pretty full, and the waiter at the door has a nice smile. All of this I keep to myself.

Once we sit, Nelly wants to eat something like she ate in Barcelona last year when she visited for one week. Nellie wonders about the salads. Then they go for something safe like potatoes. I think I order sardines. Although nobody makes a comment about my choice, I feel a kind of disapproval or maybe just distaste. Then I think that sometimes I feel things that are not real because I might have an outsider complex.

After lunch it's Spanish nap time, but we wander in a state of wonder and jet lag through the quiet streets. I won't remember, later, what we talk about or what is going through my head as we wait to see everything come back to life. But as the four of us stroll the narrow streets and I raise my iPhone to take pictures of the cupolas, cornices, steeples, railings, columns or just simple statues along my way, I have a feeling of awe that I will remember, of being baffled to be on this journey, similar to many I have taken before and yet so unlike any of them.

At 4 p.m., everything and everybody in Leon, as everywhere in Spain, wakes up. We walk towards the Cathedral de Leon, but before we get there, we see this other building. One that stops me in my tracks. It has angular towers on each corner, like a fairytale castle, lobulated arches on its windows, a gray stone façade. Gothic, I think. The lintel above the entrance door reads "Casa de Botines," and it is crowned with a stone statue: a hooded warrior, a templar perhaps, killing an animal that at first sight looks like a crocodile. Later I'll read about it and learn that this is Saint George slaying the dragon. But now I search for words and can't find any for the jump in my heart, how from inside my chest a smile rises, crinkles the sides of my eyes. "Gaudi!" I scream.

I think of Barcelona, the times I went there with my husband when we would wander forever inside and outside the buildings designed by Gaudi. We were amazed by the twisted turrets, the rounded balconies, it felt like a museum amuse-ment park. And later, when we went with our kids, the image of them running around Park Güell. Gaudi, this incredible Catalan architect who used exuberant color and free flowing curved shapes to form structures that seem to belong to an imaginary world.

"I didn't know," I say.

I wasn't expecting this, I guess I didn't research before-hand: Gaudi was here. He came from Astorga (oh, we will be there, too!) to Leon to build a residence, a house with a warehouse for the owners of a fabric company. From such an ordinary commission, this magical world. Medieval air, neo-Gothic details, small niches. Diaphanous, sheer illumination for practical ventilation, lobulated doors and even a sculpture of Saint George slaying the dragon. When we enter the *Casa de Botines*, I'm mesmerized. I touch, although I shouldn't, the varnished wood of the doors, the stair banisters. I watch the light diffused by translucent glass or the stained-glass win-dows. And while I'm joyful in this present, I'm also in the past, as the memories of Barcelona, the Gaudi buildings, the park, all that we admired as we played together, so many years ago, keep flooding my brain.

My friends are almost as excited as I am. This house, with its mirrors, stairs, and many small rooms with narrow win-dows overlooking the plaza, makes us all feel like children. It's a playground for grown-ups.

Once we come out, almost in a daze, there is more — to see, to gather, to take in before we go shopping, have another meal — more to fall in love with: a Cathedral (I don't go in, I have seen enough), a museum, a chapel, the pictures accumu-late, my brain storage capacity is not enough. Thus, our presump-tions, our hopes, for today, have panned out.

First Day of Walking

Leon to Villadangos
del Paramo, Spain

May 1, 2019

The iconic signposts of the Way of Saint James

Why We Don't Take a Taxi

On the train, on our way to Leon, we had discussed, argued, deliberated, and planned how we'd start the walk. "I read that there's nothing to see until we get to the end of the city of Leon. We might as well take a taxi to the start of the real hike," says Nellie.

"We can take a few pictures at the start, check if there is something of interest before we take the taxi," I say.

After a while, we all agreed. Why waste energy on a walk on pavement and asphalt, between stores and apartments, masonry, brickwork, instead of enjoying the trail?

"It will be our first day, we better take it easy,"

I think it's Margaret who says this. Nelly nods. We have had this conversation before.

We leave the hotel at 8:30 a.m., full of energy, adrenalin, excitement and begin to follow the yellow arrows[3], signposts that point the way to Santiago, some 330 kilometers, 205 miles away. We find our first yellow arrow painted on the concrete wall of a corner building, a gray shell embedded above it. The shell is another symbol of the El Camino pilgrimage. We notice that most of the other hikers we see on our way carry one of these shells hanging from their backpack or their shorts.

"I want to buy one of those shells and hang it from my backpack," says Nelly, as soon as we discover that those would identify us as "pilgrims." We all agree that we should buy the

---

3. The yellow arrows along El Camino are iconic signposts to indicate the right way at tricky crossroads. Except for the concrete signposts set up by the cities, they are mainly painted by hand and are sometimes difficult to see or non-existent, as many of them are maintained by volunteers.

shells, although I'd thought that our boots, hats, trekking poles, full backpacks and general demeanor would already give us away.

After a few blocks, we find an open store that sells knick knacks. I laugh about the eagerness of my companions as they go through the baskets full of shells, looking for the perfect shell, but in the end I succumb. Thus, today, I carry a seashell attached to a clip dangling from a pocket on the back of my royal blue backpack. It makes a dull noise with each step and I think that this is how my dog must feel with the tag attached to his collar.

We find our second arrow attached to a pole. The yellow sign is painted on an intense blue background and it's easy to see when we cross a street. But the third arrow is a hand-painted one on the pavement that we wouldn't have noticed were we not, frantically, looking for it. We discover that these markers come in all shapes and forms, including some nice blocks of stone with the shell sign and the number of kilometers left to get to Santiago. We learn to be on the lookout for them, happy when we see them, because that means we didn't get lost, we are on the right path.

It is early and the streets are deserted, the air clean, the sky white and blue. We stroll for the first few blocks, we stop and admire the buildings, we find things we hadn't seen the day before. This is a different part of the city. We take pictures, and we walk. Soon, we have been walking for an hour. Should we take the taxi? someone asks. "Let's walk a bit more, this is nice, we have energy," I say.

So, we walk, and soon we have walked two hours, maybe three. Why take a taxi now? We seem to be doing fine. Nellie doubts, but Nelly would like to walk the whole thing, although she'll bend to the will of the rest of us. "We shouldn't cheat... but this is the first day, so maybe it's OK to take a taxi," she says. But none of us makes the effort to look for one. There are no taxis going around, we'd have to ask. Thus, and because we can, we do, we walk all the way, our boots striding the streets, crossing a bridge, until we get to the beginning of a trail. Even if I think that Nellie doesn't quite agree, and Margaret wonders if we are wise, I'm fine. I like to walk through cities and stare at the shops, even if they are just hardware stores, and at all the passersby, to imagine where are they are going and if they are locals or foreigners like us. I'm content, we are finally on our way.

Follow the Yellow Arrow

55

I walk the path,
follow the yellow arrows.

Inside my head:

Caminante no hay Camino,
Wayfarer, walker, there is no path

One step, another,
I look, I observe, I talk
to myself,
to the women I walk with.

Why do I walk?

I follow the path,
the yellow arrows,
the *conchas*,
pointing the way.

From where we are,
from where we start,
in Leon,
in Leon y Castilla,
Galicia,
in Northern Spain.
I follow the path,
to Santiago.

Inside my head:

Who am I?
I'm a mother,
spouse, daughter,
worker, maker,
walker.
Who am I?

Woman, I reply
to myself,
there is no longer
someone pointing the way,
you decide.

One step, the next,
kilometers down the road.
I look for a sign,
a flower, a plant,
a face or a pair of eyes,
to point, to illuminate the path,
let me know,
where to go.

No illumination, not yet,
so instead,
I just walk.

The trail, the gravel,
the road.
The noise of my steps,
the chaos of voices

inside my head.

Caminante,
allí está el Camino.
There is the road.

Stop and watch.

The blue sky, bright yellow sun,
two storks
make a nest
on top of the old church.

Stop and listen.

Trucks on the road,
the chirping of many birds,
boots against the gravel.

Stop and taste.

In the air,
olives and rosemary,
gasoline and fertilizer.

Stop and touch.

The stone
that is part of the wall
from long ago,
cold, unyielding.

Now continue,
carry the road with you,
a picture here,
a word after.

Caminante,
allí está el Camino.

You made it,
you've arrived.
At the end of this road,
there is another road,
now depart.

Follow the yellow arrows,
the shells, the *conchas*,
home.

Flower Child - 1969

Humid summer, yellow and green striped bell-bottoms, glass pipes and bongs in head shop windows, red flowers braided into her waist-length hair. She holds her lover's hand as they walk side by side through a rainbow of primary colors. Boho vests mix with plaid shorts or the psychedelic patterns of the long skirts. The sounds of "Like a Rolling Stone" coming from inside a record store. She watches and listens, detects the pungent, musky smell unbeknownst to her until then, unable to believe she now inhabits this utopian world.

Birkenstocks on their feet, they walk to their car, a magical blue 1960 Pontiac convertible with blue leather seats, that goes fast on the new highways. She stands up on the bucket seat, on the passenger side, while her lover drives, oblivious to the rules of the road, invulnerable to danger. A white blouse embroidered with hummingbirds flowing in the wind. The promised land, a world of possibility ahead.

When the future comes, she will always remember this feeling inside herself.

When she was a child, she wished to be Doris Day, to live in that enchanted land of the movies. She sang "que será será," ignorant of the meaning of its lyrics, or the plot of the movie in which it was first sung. In her mind, she saw a knight in shining armor, the "principe azul," who would come and lift her onto his white horse, take her to America, North America. A land of bright colors under a sunny sky.

She remembers her wish when she touches his shoulder, steals a kiss. Afterwards, she sits back again on the cool leather seat next to him and imagines them riding forever towards the sunny horizon as the titles come down, The End in shiny letters.

That was before she knew that this dream she wanted to call home, this enchanted land, North America, could be gray instead of yellow or blue or red. That the magical Pontiac would be stolen, and then impounded for profit, instead of returned, by the state police. That the National guard would be called to break student protests and they would see military uniforms entering a university, again.

Pontiac, December 1968

I: A Secret Friend – Unwritten Rules

We act by unwritten rules. Rules that we absorb from what is left unsaid, or from the subtle way in which it's said, or rules we make up ourselves, because those we love, we don't want to hurt.

The boy I had chosen to date was educated, quite handsome, respectful, gentle and kind. He was a good listener, and his worst habit was cigarette smoking, something that most people I knew at that time also did. My father was a chain smoker himself and he had always enjoyed quiet, knowledgeable people. So why was I so convinced that he would disapprove of my choice? Why did I believe that it would distress and upset him to know I was dating Enrique?

I lost my mother too young to have a chance to talk about boys with her, and my father didn't know how, or maybe he found it awkward to discuss dating or boyfriends with his very young and only daughter. He did warn me to be suspicious of strangers, but he never forbade me to go out with any of my friends. He would only plead that I be home early. Every evening I went out with friends he would repeat the same words:

"I worry when it's late and you're not home."

And I would repeat the same answer: "Don't worry, someone will walk me home. Don't stay up."

But my father would stay up. At that time, we lived in the only apartment on the sixth floor of a six-floor building and most of the time, when I got back late at night, I would see him waiting for me with the door open before I was out of the elevator. I felt guilty. I knew, or I thought I knew, that if I dated someone who was outside the tribe, not a part of the Jewish community, I would betray my father. He was a secular Jew who believed in family and traditions, in going once a year to the synagogue. I thought that my dating choice would make him angry and make him sad. I started to lie. I told myself it was a white lie.

The boy I had started to date had been raised Catholic, but didn't believe in any religion, and I thought he was a paragon of virtue. However, I believed that I had to hide his presence in my life from most of the people I loved. I was wrong, but I was also a tad right.

I first met Enrique at the new building of the Facultad de Ciencias Exactas, Físicas y Naturales of the Universidad de Buenos Aires[4]. It was 1965 and the inside of the building was still being finished, but some of the advanced math evening classes were held there. The edifice was part of a new University campus that had been under construction for a while and was modern and state of the art. The blackboards were green instead of black, screens could be pulled down to show "viewgraphs," and the classrooms were designed as amphitheaters where all the seats were made of smooth light-colored wood and had wide arm rests.

The first time I met Enrique, I was in my sophomore year, and I was taking a third-year math class for physics majors. I was a shy seventeen-year-old, who was still quite unsure of who she was but who found assurance in math and science. I think that because I was a focused student and had learned early to not slouch, I looked mature and self-confident to the exterior world, even if my brain was always in turmoil.

The new University building was pretty much empty of people and furniture, except for a few classrooms where classes were being held, and the offices for the professors and assistant

---

4. School of Exact Sciences, Physics and Natural Sciences. It is the University of Buenos Aires that focuses only on math, physics, chemistry, and biology.

teachers on both sides of a long hall at one end of the building. There was a temporary bar outside of the classrooms. Just a counter where we could drink espresso and eat small pastries — a basic need in my hometown for students and teachers alike. On a break from my class, I made a space for myself at the crowded counter to order an espresso. I had only ten minutes until the class started again. I watched the harried bartender fill the little cup while I listened to the background noise of the many students around me chatting away. My brain giggled when I heard a male voice next to me say something about a cowlick in his hair.

"I plaster it with water, but it just springs back up," the voice said.

"Just put a net on it when you sleep," someone else said with a laugh.

It wasn't a serious conversation; they were horsing around, but I didn't quite get that. My social skills were not well developed, and I was curious. I turned my head to see the hair they were talking about. Beside me, leaning on the counter, I saw a tall and thin, attractive, curly-haired blonde young man. On the way to the cowlick, my eyes stopped at a pair of strange blue eyes. They had amber spots inside a deep blue sky. Surprising my timid self, I didn't hesitate to interject my voice in the middle of a conversation that was not mine.

"Just let it be. Cowlicks are fun. Make people think you're a troublemaker. Like Daniel el travieso,"[5] I said and, to dissimulate my diffidence, I attempted a quirky grin.

He turned away from his companion and watched me for a moment before he said, "What class are you in?" His face had a smile that I found not insulting but kind. Thus, instead of resorting to my habitual reserve and silence, I found myself gabbing all through the break with this unusual guy who was four years my senior and looked like a priest in his dark suit, white shirt, black leather shoes and skinny black tie. I got back

---

5. Denice (Danny) the menace

late to class and felt very grown up.

He seemed to know the ins and outs of the new building. He had told me with a wink that the offices of the professors and the graduate assistants were finished, but they had not yet been assigned, so in the meantime he was studying, really trespassing, in one. Would I want to check it out the next time I was in the building? I could do my homework there if I wanted.

One week later, in the early afternoon, I plucked up my courage and walked the long corridors of the new building. "I just want to check the new offices," I told myself as I ambled the hallway between the empty spaces that still smelled of paint. As I looked inside each unoccupied room, I could feel the sweat collect under my armpits and prayed it would not leave stains on my blouse. Although my conscious mind believed that I was just going to explore the building, my unconscious understood a different motivation. That afternoon I had dressed with extra care.

Once I found the office where a blond guy, him, was sitting behind a large desk, I didn't know what to do. He held a cigarette in one hand and a book with the other. There was a large ashtray, full of stubs, sitting on the glass desktop. Before I could say a word, he noticed my presence hovering near the door and waved me in. "Hola, bienvenida a mi oficina," he said with a chuckle. Of course, it wasn't his office, but I was welcome. Many years afterwards, he told me how striking I had looked to him at that moment.

I was dressed in a black and red plaid miniskirt, a white short-sleeved blouse, had a thin black cashmere sweater over my shoulders, and my legs were encased in black fishnet pantyhose. I carried my books inside a large purse that hung from my shoulder and I was holding a cigarette between two of my fingers. My face was full of freckles, my hair was sunlit and very long, and although I gave the appearance of extreme self-assurance, I remember how insecure, how hesitant and uncertain of myself I felt. I stood next to the desk and looked at *the walls and at the new green chalk boards as I wondered what to say. A janitor dressed in a gray apron and carrying a tray with little cups appeared next to me at the door.*

"Do you guys want some coffee?" he said. Yes, it was still a time when that happened, at least at the University of Buenos Aires. His question broke the uncomfortable moment, and I was able to open my mouth and emit a sound. "Yes, thank you," I said, and when I heard another yes I picked two cups from the tray and I carried them with precarious balance to the desk.

After that, Enrique and I started to chat: first we talked about the quality of the coffee (terrible), then the office decoration (excellent), the new building (really nice), and the old one that both of us loved and where I was still taking most of my classes. I got weary of standing there on the other side of the desk and sat down across from him, in the only other chair. I took out a notebook and made like I was doing homework, but we kept talking and I was distracted. When he learned my class schedule, he said he might have to go downtown near the old University building and could look for me at the end of my classes. Maybe we could go somewhere for tea and pastries. It wasn't a date, and I wasn't sure he even meant it, the part about looking for me.

And yet, less than one week later, on Friday, December 13, as I stepped out from the threshold of the ancient wooden entrance to the University building, I had a jolt. I saw him leaning against the concrete wall, a cigarette in one hand, a book in the other.

"Do you want to go somewhere for coffee or tea?" he said, as if it were the most natural thing in the world that he would be waiting for me there.

That was the beginning. We sat at one of the round marble tables of a corner café, chatted for a long time, then he walked me back to my house. We kissed. We began to date, and I hid our dates, and him from my father. For a while, I even hid what he meant for me from myself.

End of First Hiking Day - Beer, Not Wine

When did it change? When was it that what had seemed as if it would last forever wasn't there anymore? When did we stop walking on pavement and welcome the gravel underfoot? I think it was after we walked over a small bridge, in awe of the sudden beauty after so much concrete gray: the water reflecting the clouds under the Spanish sunlight, the small park with red and yellow flowers, an air of cheerfulness around us. It was after crossing that bridge that we couldn't find a yellow arrow and we walked in circles, confused, and we had to ask for directions.

I don't remember the actual crossing into a different world, one with trees and grass, no stores or houses, just a small church sometimes and very few humans around. However, I do know that, although we were tired, our steps lightened at the sight of the trail, and we broke into sighs of relief when we saw the first sign indicating that the next town — Villadangos del Paramo, an unusual name for American ears — was just a mile or so away. What I can't forget is the moment when, after we finally found our small hotel with our bags inside it, and we took our showers, three of us met downstairs for a pre-dinner celebratory drink. Nelly preferred to rest in her room until dinner.

I usually drink wine, red wine, but that evening something took hold of me and I ordered the house beer. As the liquid traveled through my body, my spirit lifted. "Is this what you expected?" asked Margaret. I don't know what I expected. A part of me expected adventure, different landscapes, the thrill of travel and of seeing new places. But I think a hidden part of me also expected some kind of miracle, an epiphany, a revelation of who I was, who I had become. I told her that, so far, I was content with what I got. And although we chatted away until dinner, the three of us couldn't quite put into words our thoughts about the day.

Later, the four of us sat at the table for a meal of fish, Spanish salad and bread. "I have never tasted bread so good as this," almost all of us said in unison. Of course, our unaccustomed bodies hungered for carbohydrates after so many kilometers on foot. This time I had a glass of red wine. I celebrated having survived the first day of hiking. We could do this. We would do this; it wasn't so hard.

Expectation and Annoyance

Villadangos del Paramo to Astorga, Spain

May 2, 2019

Entering Hospital d'Orbigo

I'm Quiñonas at Via Hospital d'Orbigo

Today we will walk 20 miles. We start around 8:30 a.m., while the air is still cool, our early morning energy rippling the air. We are dressed in layers. The puff jacket, the wick-away-perspiration blue merino sweater, even the t-shirt — I have a black tank top underneath — come off as the sun rises and we walk, mile after mile, for three hours.

Ready for an early lunch by 11 a.m., or maybe 11:30 a.m., we enter Hospital d'Orbigo, the guidebook-recommended spot to stop. An idyllic village with medieval buildings and a legend that shaped a fictional story. I learn about the story later. I don't know much about the town as we enter. I'm just enthralled by the long bridge over the blue-green stream of water leading to it. Hypnotized, I watch the backdrop of a narrow street path, red-tiled-roofed houses and greenery, and listen to the quiet.

The four of us, the two N's and two M's, walk in single file over gray tiles, a path between cobblestones, in the middle of the 200-meter-long bridge that crosses the Orbigo River. This is the gate to the city.

I walk at the back of the line as my brain grasps, digests and works to absorb what I hear, what I see, what I feel, as my feet ask for a rest after the first 9 miles of the day. My eyes watch the shape of the arches that hold the bridge aloft and the background of sky and clouds that turn in a moment from gray to steel and back to white. Except for us four, there are no other humans in sight, and I want to focus on the sound of the breeze brushing the water, the railing, my hair, and the quiet calm of the town ahead. But I can't filter out the prattle of the women walking ahead of me. Right now, I want to be present. I want to observe, I want to embrace the moment, feel the breeze, and I want to learn.

"How many calories did we already burn?" "How many steps?" "What does your Fitbit say? My Apple watch..." A chat about protein, sleep, body needs. I grow anxious, I lose my sense of purpose.

I'm not all that spiritual, but this long walk, this landscape, invites me to transcend, to become someone else, and I feel annoyed at these women who seem fixated on the number of steps or if this long walk will help them to lose weight. Well, I think, to calm my inner self, I guess you can make anything into a higher purpose. After all, I also carry a Fitbit and check it at the end of the day. But right now, I want to observe in peace, keep this story inside my head. As always, I feel I'm an outsider. I tend to be always out of step with my friends.

I first notice the beautiful calligraphy in red and black on a large display just as we enter the city and I want to stop to read what it says. It is a discovery, a welcome surprise, when I learn from it about the legend of the bridge. I have to read fast because my companions keep walking ahead in search of a place to have lunch, while I stay in place, mesmerized by the tale.

Once upon a time, around 1434, there was a knight and author by the name of Suero de Quiñones who fell deeply in love with a lady. Because she didn't seem to return his affections, he thought of a way to impress her. He declared himself imprisoned by his love and fought with his right arm bared against the Moors in Grenada. When the lady still didn't requit his love, Suero wore an iron choker and occupied the Orbigo bridge with the help of nine fellow knights, demanding a fight from any man who wanted to cross the bridge. Suero swore to break 300 lances before moving on. The event concluded with a solemn ceremony after thirty days, when they removed the iron collar that symbolized Suero's love bondage, as he was so badly injured that he couldn't joust anymore. It turns out that the absurdity of this story of chivalry gone awry gave Cervantes his idea for his fictional Don Quixote, who went out to fight for his divine lady. Don Quixote declared himself to be a direct descendant of the man who killed Suero.

I fall in love with the bizarre and romantic story and forget my petty annoyances. I imagine one of my trekking poles as my sword and think of who I can joust with along my way. I'm Quiñonas, I'll fight for justice, or maybe just to conquer this Camino, this trail. Maybe, also, my relations with others and myself.

Then it is time to eat. We're all so hungry that we consume eggs, ham, a seventeen-ingredient salad and all the bread. "The egg sandwiches seem a good choice." Nellie says. I have this sense that my companions think I'm difficult when I spend time discussing with the waiter, in Spanish, the ingredients of the salad.

"How can you discuss a salad?" Nelly says, and I notice reproaching glances. They are hungry and want to eat but discussing how a dish is made is a pleasure I grew up with.

The sandwiches are simple, although they look Instagram-picture-ready: the egg is embedded in a hole on top of the bread. The salad is a mess of color and a mix of sweet, sour and salty tastes, but doesn't photograph well. Do we order who we are?

While the other three have ordered egg sandwiches, I eat the complex salad.

I Smile at Pain

Because I'm perceived
as aloof, as if
I brush off the words.
Because I can hide
my emotions, look strong.
Because I don't cry
and I smile a lot,
it is assumed that I can easily
deal with reproach,
that I can manage pain.
But I can't.
It is an attitude,
maybe the arrogance
some of us learn
if we have to mother ourselves
after we turn ten.

On the Way to Astorga

Later, I think that it's all about the emotions I feel. It's so pretty, so amazing, so European, the idyllic green grass, the yellow wildflowers. The river between the dark green trees, the cobblestone streets or the red soil trails, undulating up and down. I smell olives and fish, even if the air is odorless. A breeze or the hot sun, depending on the clouds that move around and turn from white to gray, steel gray, and back to white.

I march and think about how to describe a walk. A simple walk, on sore feet, 28 kilometers today. A climb of 20 kilometers the next day. Or just this. One step at a time with a mantra inside my head. *One, two, three, uno, dos, tres*, to keep the pace. Among women who sometimes are my friends and sometimes could be strangers I've just met.

After we leave Hospital d'Orbigo, we pass a town where the guide says that we should stop, but we don't. The "guide" is this thin booklet with information about the routes to follow that the company who moves our bags from hotel to hotel gave us on the first day. But none of us is very good at following directions and sometimes the routes don't make sense, at least not to us. Thus, we keep walking because we think that there are a couple more towns where we can stop before a long stretch marked on the map that seems bereft of cafes. But there are no more towns for another eight kilometers.

So far today we have already walked 45,000 steps or so. (We now count steps instead of kilometers or miles, it makes us feel like champions of a secret contest.) And we are not "there" yet. "There" being Astorga, our final destination for the day. However, we think that, once we get to the next town, San Justo de la Vega, and rest for a bit, we'll have only one more hour to go, and will get to Astorga in time for a shower, a walk through the town and a leisurely dinner. As always, we could be overly optimistic or mistaken about distances and times.

"This is easy but a bit too long," I say to my companions, but really to the air. My voice doesn't project well, and I am always carrying on a conversation with myself. I don't think they've heard what I said, which is just as well.

We've walked most of the afternoon on a red clay trail, surrounded by dark green pines, tall blades of grass and a few yellow wildflowers. Now, just after I've uttered my comment, there is a steep descent. The trail has changed and we need to hike over small slippery stones — not hard, but a minor challenge. I looked towards the horizon and see the steeple of a church in the nearby small town rising into an intense blue and white sky. It's a cliché, but most of the time, the Spanish sky does look as if a hidden hand has drawn the well-defined edges of the clouds that fly above us. Sometimes they resemble animals, and sometimes they stretch out and form a thick white and silver blanket that covers the sun and cools the air around us. I know these clouds are just accumulations of minute droplets of water, or ice crystals suspended in the air. I even know their names, *cumulus, stratocumulus*. But I like to imagine that they are rabbits or little lambs, or white kitties, a doggy perhaps. They have secret wings and play hide and seek while they watch us from the sky. I remember to look back down at the trail before I take another step. The small rocks have a way of moving under my feet, making me trip.

A half hour later, we have finished our descent. I point towards a sign that reads San Justo de la Vega."

"We should stop to pee here," I say. We have learned that we should stop and pee at any place on our path that has a restroom. We've learned from experience on several occasions when we've had to hide in the bushes to relieve ourselves. Sometimes, there are no bushes around. Margaret agrees and we walk a bit off the trail to find a small café. We go inside and Margaret buys a small bottle of water and I order an espresso. Although there are no rules in most of these places against using the restrooms if you are a pilgrim, we feel we should buy something to use them.

When we return to the trail, we walk at first on red soil between borders of lush vegetation. But sometime later that green opulence disappears. Instead, there is a dirt track and dry empty fields surround us. We notice some buildings nearby that resemble warehouses and some private houses. There's no longer a trail.

Margaret and I look at each other. I see in her a mirror of myself: the hiking pants and the boots covered with dirt of the trail, the sweaty t-shirt, the blue backpack with a first aid kit and extra clothes (by now, the backpacks are almost empty of water and snacks). Most of all, I know she has the same tired eyes I do, hidden behind her dark glasses.

"The gate to Astorga should be nearby," Margaret says. I nod.

We know that, in this part of Spain, the gates to the villages are sometimes elusive, and there is always a long way from the gate to the hotel. Entrances to the towns are marked most of the time with a map, or a sign, but sometimes it is just a change in the scenery that gives them away. This time there is nothing, except a tall, maybe four-story high footbridge and a cliff far away. I point to what looks like structures on top of the cliff.

"Would that be Astorga?" I ask.

"That's too far," Margaret says. We are fatigued, we want to sit and rest, but there are only weeds and empty fields all around us.

In the meantime, the two N's have walked ahead, as usually happens at the end of the hiking day. Margaret and I lag behind, taking our time, while they forge ahead, focused on getting to the hotel earlier and being able to rest before dinner. So, it's just the two of us, the two M's, wondering aloud if we have lost our way. We are the only two persons in the middle of nowhere.

We walk around and look for the yellow arrows, or the shells, the pointers to El Camino, the St. James Way. We need to see them to feel confident we are on the right path. These markers always make us smile. Either painted by hand, scratched on concrete with a piece of chalk or sculpted on more modern cement markers that show how many kilometers to reach 0, at Finisterre, the end of the earth. The markers always point the way.

"Where was the last one we saw?" I ask. I'm uneasy, I think that last marker was a while ago. We walk in a circle and look around until, when we are about to give up, we find a small, white arrow, hand scratched in chalk, that points towards the bridge. The arrow is white instead of yellow and the bridge looks to be one kilometer away. I begin to doubt that that is the right way. I take out the small map from the travel agency that I carry in my pocket. It is not very detailed and, although we can find Astorga and San Justo de la Vega, we can't find on the map the spot where we stand now.

Margaret and I are worn-out, it has been a long day. If we follow the direction of the small arrow, we will have to walk half a mile, go up a long staircase and climb a cliff at the end. Is the city really up there, so far away? We don't want to walk up and then have to come back. We decide that before embarking on the steep climb that might not get us to where we were going, we could try to check against Google maps on our phones. The application doesn't usually work well in these out of the way areas, but maybe it will this time and will help us decide. The Google map also directs us towards the bridge and also informs us that there is another hour-and-a-half walk to the hotel.

"This is too depressing," Margaret says. We're almost there, and not anywhere near there yet.

"I don't see another option," I say.

Weary, we start to walk. We are crossing a railway track in the middle of a field covered with dry grass and wildflowers when we see an elderly guy walking ahead of us. This is the first human we have seen in a while. He has a bunch of red wildflowers in one hand and a walking stick in the other. I hurry ahead and, out of breath, ask him in Spanish if we are on the right way to Astorga.

"Where are you going?" he says.

"To the Gaudi Hotel," I say. Afterwards, I'm surprised that there was no hesitation in my mind about the potential risk of asking or telling this man where we are going, even if we are in the middle of a field, no one else in sight. Margaret walks up next to me and I feel her silent concern. We have been taught to be wary of strangers on a solitary road. However, when the guy smiles and says, "Follow me," I do.

He is dressed in sweatpants, a ragged jacket, an old dark blue cap on his head; he has an unkempt beard, and for god's sake, he carries a bunch of wildflowers as if it were a dainty bouquet, and a heavy walking stick. He could be homeless, a crazy, a psychopath, take us the wrong way, beat us with the stick to get our money. But I also know that initial perceptions based on our own biases and fears can be wrong. When we start, I like his mild-mannered way of walking and talking. He tells us about the land we are traversing. I decide that we are safe. He seems to be a nice man.

The wildflowers he carries are for his house; he walks 15 or 20 kilometers every day and has always picked them to take to his wife. But she died last year, and now he just picks them to honor her. He shows us a shortcut. We won't have to climb the foot bridge and then go up for another hour after all. He chats with me in Spanish while we walk.

When we enter the city, he points to a painted wall on a

Random encounter with a kind man

building that sits next to an empty lot. "One of the many Astorga frescos. It represents the war of Spain against France," he says. We turn our heads and look up to appreciate the colorful painting that covers the whole side of the building. Then he points to another building less than a block away that has cylindrical towers and looks like a medieval castle.

"That is the Gaudi palace. It was built with gray granite from El Bierzo. The arches at the entrance have a pointed apex, like an arabesque. And look at those pointed chimneys," he says. "It is just across from your hotel!"

Our weariness is gone. We don't feel the time pass or our tired feet as we walk and learn the story of the town and bits and pieces of the life of this stranger we met along our path. I'm surprised when I notice that it took us forty minutes to get to the hotel instead of the predicted hour-and-a-half.

I haven't gotten the name of this man, but he's told us he's lived in Astorga for 50 years, and that now he is retired. He is 68 years old and when we enter the city itself, many people greet him and stop for a short chat. He must be a city icon.

Once at the hotel door, before he leaves, I ask to take a selfie with him and the bright wildflowers. He has lightened our day. Margaret and I have forgotten how disheartened we had felt not that long ago.

Once I'm up in my room, I take a long shower, wash my panties, pants, t-shirt, and socks, and I'm ready to go down for dinner in less than an hour. It is surprising how quick I can be when I travel!

During dinner, we tell the N's about our adventure and show them our selfie with the guy holding the bunch of wild-flowers. The N's recount their walk up the bridge and around to get to the hotel, still ahead of us.

Selfie with a kind man

Short Evening in Astorga

We have a single night in Astorga and, as it's turned out, no afternoon promenade. We've gotten here too late. However, not everything is lost: we have an amazing dinner for our amazing hunger after so much walking. Me: grilled prawns with salad and a Dorada fish, also grilled and with more salad. Nellie and Margaret: oxtail with asparagus (oxtail was my husband Enrique's favorite, but I am no longer eating meat, mostly just fish). Nelly: a mix of salmon, prawn and two other fish. Wine, *natilla* for dessert with a *mantecado*, a type of pastry that I learned to love in Argentina when I was a child. It is typical of the area of Castilla and Leon.

Astorga is a nice, large, busy city with the Gaudi Palace and our hotel across from it. After dinner, we all want to go out, stroll through the town. We wish we could go and check out the Episcopal Palace of Astorga and the magnificent building designed by Gaudi. It is just across from the hotel, tempting us with its turrets, its gothic ogival arches, moat, rounded stone walls — a castle for us children to play in, but it is too late. Our minds wish, but our bodies reject the wish, demanding rest instead.

"We should have stayed at least two days here," Nellie says, and Nelly agrees.

"But you said you needed to be home in 17 days," says Margaret. We planned the trip so Nelly could leave in time to get back for a board meeting. Although Margaret and I will stay another day at the end, we won't have enough time to stop and relish the beauty of some of the towns we'll pass through — and have to keep passing, in order to recover our bags at the next hotel. "Next time," I say, and we go back inside and sleep the sleep of the almost dead. Tomorrow is another day, and we've planned to at least walk around, look at the outside of the Palace of Gaudi, the Cathedral, before starting our long trek to the next city: Rabanal.

Conquer Fear

Astorga to Rabanal
del Camino, Spain

May 3, 2019

Red soil trail

Mind Games

As I walk
this defiant pilgrim's trail,
as I hike
over mud and grass,
I search

for a mystical revelation,
a magical burst of light
even though I don't believe
in divine life.

Of course,
it doesn't come.

Instead, today,
I sustain my pace
with endless mind games.

Today,
I'll conquer fear.
Fear of the unknown,
fear of being alone,
fear of pain.

Maybe, I tell myself,
I'll recover the wonder
from long ago.

Marvel at nature,
eliminate the dread
of the snow-capped mountains,
and the clear rivers
I must cross.

I'll listen
to the chirping of the birds,
the cuckoo far away.
The sound of the breeze,
blowing between the fields,
of wheat, barley, maybe chard.

I'll watch, amazed, as we walk past
 the many shades of green,
or those rows of gargoyles,
the pruned trunks
of dormant vines,
standing in the red soil,
waiting for their crowns of leaves,
to become grapes, wine.

Still, my hands encased
in fingerless gloves,
grasp, grip, clench
the trekking poles.

But I keep going,
I hike, I march, I play a mantra,
inside my head:
one, two, one,
one, two, three.
Uno, dos, tres.

This way I conquer fear,
I conquer pain,
to bear
the long distance
still ahead.

Goodbye Astorga, Hello Rabanal

It took us part of the early morning to leave Astorga, we wanted so much to stay, to walk inside the Palace, the Cathedral; but we had to be satisfied with wandering around for just over an hour, taking pictures, hoping we would be back another time. Then we walked. We thought it might be an easy walk, since on the map it looked to be shorter than the previous day's hike and it seemed to run through a simple country landscape. We hiked between green fields, meeting almost no one on the way. A few houses every so often, maybe a café to take a bathroom break.

We stepped in twos, sometimes in fours or singly to change the pace. We chatted about Astorga, our hopes for the rest of the year. Nellie might want to retire once her current project is completed. I said that I want to make more bracelets, it makes me happy to work with my hands after so many years of using my brain. Nellie said she had lots of beads from her sister, who had recently passed away. Then we commented on the weather, cool and sunny and dry, the beauty of the landscape. We drank water, ate snacks, and went at a relaxed pace until we got within two kilometers of Rabanal del Camino. In what by now seemed to be the usual challenge at the end of the day, the path became steep and full of rocks and roots. It was time to pay attention, or, for me, to focus on my trekking poles and where I planted each foot. And yet, the pines to each side of the trail helped to keep my interest and make me forget pain, effort, anything else that was not a sort of joy, perhaps happiness. The pines looked like the trees in those postcards we send friends or family to remind them about the magnificence of nature. The tree needles had as many different hues of green as I have ever seen. I lack adjectives to describe the emotions that I felt, or the light that illuminated everything on our way.

Although several portions of the trail were uphill, the path was shorter than in previous days, and for once we got to our destination early in the afternoon. It was about 4:30 p.m. when we arrived at the gates to the city, so we had time for a drink before dinner, and for me, for a walk around town. I'm always curious, even when my body is tired, and my feet might hurt, about who lives in these small, very old villages, with no automobiles and narrow cobblestone alleys, rather than roads.

Rabanal turned out to be a very small and quaint town with two small stores and maybe 50 houses built of brown brick or stone. There are three small churches. The parish church is also small, barren of decoration, with the large towers associated with Romanesque architecture. It was supposed to have some Knights Templar connection. I have seen so many town churches on our way that I ignored the details of this one, at first, until I looked up and saw the bird's nests on the steeple top and the large storks nesting there. I found the image dissonant and harmonious at the same time; it made me smile.

As I wandered the many narrow streets, I stopped to admire and take pictures of a wooden carved door opening to a courtyard and the many wildflowers growing in assorted containers at random spots in the street. I have a whole collection of pictures of the elaborately carved doors that have always fascinated me when I travel. Each one reminds me of the entrance to a fairy tale, or to a life of different possibilities. Is there a story behind these complex engravings? All of the entrance doors to the various places where I've lived have been unremarkable. I think that they hid my stories, in the same way that my outer persona hides my internal emotions, still. But I'm learning.

The Rabanal streets were quiet, no people milling around. I entered a store that sold knick-knacks, but after looking around, exchanging a couple of niceties with the merchant and touching everything in sight, I didn't buy anything. My sons say that touching but not buying is a very bad habit of mine. "One day they will throw you out of the store or you'll get yelled at," they say. But I need to touch to feel if something is right, if it will fill a void or perhaps a need in my life. The merchant was not angry with me. I think he was bored in the empty store and I provided some tourist entertainment. Soon I had to turn back. It was the time for dinner to be served, and I couldn't skip that.

Rabanal carved door.

Pride and Gratitude

Rabanal del Camino
to Molinaseca

May 3, 2019

Towards Molinaseca

Today's Lessons

It's the fifth day since we started our actual hike and I have had no spiritual revelations yet. Of course, my scientist brain doesn't believe in divine revelations, but rather in discoveries, recognitions based on new facts. My heart, or rather my right brain, on the other hand, likes to daydream and hopes for magic, for a vision to help me feel again.

What I have experienced so far in this trip is the joy and pride of doing this hike at my age and, in particular, the lessons I learned today. Concentrate, avoid distractions. If you are going up or down steep slopes, over rocks, roots, gravel running through a landscape of yellow and purple flowers, stay in the moment, focus on the next step. Don't look back. Eat, not just before, but during a seven-hour-straight walk. And express gratitude unremittingly. Gratitude to the Zumba and body pump classes, the gym teachers, the friend who insisted you take hikes in Palos Verdes to practice, and the friend who helped to pull you up today, when you tripped on a treacherous rock and fell, chin first, spread eagle on the white gravel path. The friend who held your back a second time when you got dizzy. Or maybe just plain gratitude to be alive. Lessons that are hard to learn.

Trip, Fall, Get Up and Go Forward

It was 3 p.m. when I fell, twice, within thirty seconds. First, I tripped, then after I stood up, lightheaded, I passed out, started to fall again, I don't remember. Margaret held my back so I didn't end up with my head on the rocks. What I know is that when my brain woke up, my eyes opened, maybe one second, maybe one minute later, I was sitting on the gravel, someone offering me water, Margaret offering me a snack.

I have to say that it was a challenging path, but not more so than others we had already done. It had up and down slopes, a mix of small white rocks and gravel that made it easy to slip and slide, but what did me in was being distracted and weak. Distracted because I kept looking back to make sure that Margaret was behind me. Weak, because I hadn't eaten since morning breakfast, waiting to find a small town where we could have lunch. I believe that the others had been snacking. But me? I'm tough. I thought, "I can wait, the town is just around the corner, I like to eat sitting down." But there was no town for several miles.

After I got up, I checked my limbs; they were working. There was blood on my chin and my cheek, probably my knee, my right-hand pinky. We scrambled with our first aid kits, finally able to put them to good use.

"Do you want to take a taxi?" Nellie and Nelly asked, although we were in the middle of nowhere and I doubt we could have found one. "No," I said. I'm stubborn and, after I fell, I had to push forward. Like the Energizer Bunny, I have this inner battery that keeps me going. Less than one hour later we finally found the town, stopped and had lunch. "Don't do that again," I chastised myself. "Never repress your hunger waiting to find the right place, eat that snack you've carried all morning! But most of all, keep your focus! Don't get distracted and look back before you look ahead. And be grateful to the friends who have your back." I guess there were a few lessons to learn there. But sometimes I'm a slow student.

Where I fell on my way to Molinaseca

One More Challenge

After lunch, I was again ready to go. We walked a few blocks and almost got lost, but the locals, with looks of surprise, showed us the way. A middle-aged woman, dressed in black, walked with us a couple of blocks to make sure we found the trail. "It is late to start," she said. We wondered, with a bit of anxiety, why she would say something like that. It was only 4 p.m.. That map seemed to show less than 10 kilometers, so it would take us at most two or three hours to walk to the hotel, and there was plenty of light ahead.

Less than half an hour later, we realized why: the path was arduous, demanding, we didn't look like spring chickens, and it might take us until later in the evening to get to the end.

The trail, if the route could be called that, had ups and downs, rocks, boulders and stones of different sizes, some very smooth and easy to slip on, sometimes a few threads of water or even a narrow stream running between or over the rocks. And yet, it was a magical landscape. Purple and yellow flowers at the sides of the path. Mountains on the horizon, a diversity of ferns and green hues, the sound of the stream. But for the last two hours of this fairytale hike, I was almost unable to enjoy the walk. I was not only tired, but anxious and fearful that the light would vanish while we were still in the middle of the rocks.

I have to admit, I prayed, or maybe I just negotiated with my non-existent God — the one I carry inside for times of need. "I promise, in exchange for safety," I said, "I promise—," and then I couldn't come up with the right thing, the right action, that would make it worthwhile to that God inside. The path was treacherous; it was getting close to 7:30 p.m. and it might soon be dark, nobody around, and we didn't know how much longer, how much harder, how much down or up to the end. As the light changed, and the shadows disappeared, the texture of the stones on the trail began to dissolve. It was more difficult to recognize the boundaries of the boulders and the rocks on our path. They were big and small, flat and rough, some arranged in the shape of stairs. Each step required total focus on every single movement, for me, to avoid injury, another fall. Time slowed down. One kilometer became 10. For those few hours, there was nothing except this path of rocks with small streams and green vegetation on the sides. An onerous, treacherous, mainly downhill path that required extreme care to avoid tripping or slipping. We wondered if we would ever get back to civilization.

Which was when this intellectual scientist, this areligious me, invented a prayer and found what could be maybe the right promise: I'll be gentler, care more about people, even those I don't like that much. Decrease the ironic, irksome remarks, learn how to keep my mouth shut.

Then the path changed to gravel, the landscape to grassy meadows, and we saw below us a road and the city sign, Molinaseca. We screamed and raised our fists in triumph, as if we had gone to the moon and back. Crazy old ladies. Fortunately, there was nobody to see us.

There was still a way to go, a bridge to cross to get to the hotel. We made it while there was still light, grateful that it was May, and at 8:30 p.m. there was still daylight. The name of the hotel was El Pecado de Josana — Josana's Sin. We hadn't committed any sins, but then, none of our names is Josana. The hotel was quite modern, with a cute guy at the desk to show us to our rooms. That brought a smile. And a glass, or maybe two, of wine to forget the pain.

To Molinaseca

Those younger than we are
might carelessly stride,
maybe even jump
from stone to stone.
I imagine,
since there is nobody on the path,
except the two of us,
struggling down the trail,
one leg, one foot at a time.

The beauty almost lost.
It's magnificent, I know.
But I can't look, can't gaze
at the luscious green all around me
as I step, step, step,
each step deliberate, and the next,
while I hold the hiking poles,
as if holding on for dear life.

Meanwhile, I worry, I calculate.
At this rate,
even if it is only two, maybe three kilometers to town,
it will take three hours,
more if one of us happens to fall.
Not an idle thought —
this morning I fell,
over jagged rocks,

distracted,
after I turned back.
I'm lucky, maybe stubborn,
or strong.
With no bones broken,
(just a gash on my chin);
five hours later,
I'm still on this trail.

Now a primitive fear sets in,
of losing strength,
of losing the
still early evening light.

My friend behind me
can't distinguish depth
after dusk.

I feel my legs quiver,
my feet become unsteady.
I can't see an end
to this steep,
uneven descent,
between dark vines,
small streams,
in the shade of the aspen trees.
But I convince myself,
I've conquered fear,
I did it during yesterday's hike.
So today, I negotiate,
with the God I don't believe in,
with the essence of myself,
with the human conscience,
with the source of creation.

I promise:
if I make it,
if I am safe,
I'll — what?
I draw a blank.
Until it comes to me,
while I try one more step,
over a large boulder,
two uneven rocks,
some mud.

I'll be more mindful,
a gentler person,
I will restrain my inner sarcasm
I will listen.
Can I change?

And then,
two minutes later,
there is a variation,
in the ragged trail.
From slippery stones, crumbling rocks, large roots
to a gentler gravel path.

We stop, look around:
a fairytale landscape,
lush green meadows,
a farmhouse on the hill,
next to it
a small blooming tree.

And before it's too late,
we see this sign on the road,
Molinaseca

Population 818.
Our fists go up,
we breathe relief,
we envision the end.

But now, I have to see,
how can I do
this gentle thing.

The "easy" part of today's hike

I Fall in the Cities I Love

At the Josana's Sin hotel, after dinner, before bed, while I check the bruise on my cheek, and smear antibiotic ointment and change the band-aid on my chin, I remember and analyze my falls. Six months ago, when I visited the city of San Miguel de Allende, Mexico, I also fell, this time crossing a street. And last year, when I stayed in the city of Austin, Texas, I fell twice, on the sidewalk. I have fallen on the path I take every day to walk the dog in my own town, and once just going up the steps to my house. I wonder if it's something I like to do in the places I love. Did I fall in Paris or Firenze? I don't remember, but I did fall walking at the top of the Cliffs of Moher near Dublin. The view was priceless. The distraction strong. My brain rewinds tape after tape of my falls and it stops at San Miguel de Allende. It is February 2018.

It was late afternoon, and I was crossing a wide street in the Guadalupe neighborhood in the town of San Miguel de Allende, Mexico, when the front of my sandal hit a fragment of pavement and I tripped. I fell across the cobble stones, between overturned pavers and concrete. My body sprawled as if I had intended to fall asleep in the middle of the street. Both hands against the white cement – once again they had stopped my head from hitting the stone, spilling my brain. My backpack still on my shoulders and the iPhone, magically intact, next to one hand. I heard a scream, a gasp, but nobody came to my aid. I wonder how I looked. Like an alcoholic? A drug addict, slumped there between pieces of concrete, dressed in a dark cotton t-shirt and flowing harem pants, and on my back, of all things, a turquoise backpack.

I cursed myself and my distraction. My age might be a big number, but I still have a fit body. I dance Zumba, lift weights, walk miles every day. So, how could I trip? Of course, my eyes were inside my mind, and my mind was inside a story I was planning to tell that evening.

I took whatever dignity I had left and, after I checked that all the body parts seemed to work, I stood up and walked to the sidewalk, lifting each leg, maintaining with effort a straight back. This ability to survive falls without permanent damage seems to be, so far, a recurrent reaction from my body.

No cars had gone by while I lay on the broken pavement, so I didn't get driven over, that was a plus to give thanks for, maybe. But there was damage. My elbow was covered in white cement and black soil, and it was bleeding, profusely. The skin of my right pinky had been peeled off and the finger was dripping blood. Whitish dust was all over my dark blue t- shirt and the dirt closed into circles the spiral designs of my Hippie Boho cotton pants. The street was covered with debris from a nearby construction site.

I wasn't wearing formal attire but had dressed in what I thought would be a fun way to be seen when I read on the stage – if my clothing hadn't been wrinkled or dirty. A friend had insisted that I should come to an open mic night and read aloud some of my writing. I'd read my work before, at workshops, but never in front of a diverse and unknown audience, on a real stage. This would be an experience, and these days I'm always willing to try something new, or different. To fall before the event, mess up my clothes, have bleeding cuts and the possibility of infection setting in, had not been in my plans.

My friend was already waiting at the Shelter Theater; it was only a few more minutes away, and I felt too stubborn to cancel. So, I looked around for a place that might have a bathroom, water, maybe band-aids. Time and space kept their *pace as if nothing had happened. The color of the sky turned dark blue, a group of schoolboys passed me by, poking and pushing each other without a look to my bleeding arm. Some merchants, done for the day, lowered their blinds. I was another speckle of grime in this world of indifference. That was when it came to me that this part of the city was different from my usual walking grounds.*

There were few stores and only small fast-food places around. This didn't look at all like the other part of town, the one where I was staying, full of tourists, interesting restaurants, art galleries and a drugstore that would have everything I needed right now. Still, I figured that a place that offered food should have a sink and water. Full of hope I entered the first small fast-food place I saw and asked. The woman behind the counter smiled."Me queda un poco," she said. How can you have a bit of water left, I wondered, until she showed me a large plastic container filled with water.

"No, no. I need clean water from a faucet." I showed her my elbow and for drama a few drops of blood fell on the counter.

"No hay." She turned the faucet handle to show me that no water was coming out.

"Dónde hay una farmacia?" I said. I saw a smile of surprise on her face when I asked in Spanish where I could find a pharmacy.

"Hacia allí," she pointed. "Not far."

It was in the opposite direction from the theater, but I didn't have a choice. I needed something to clean the wound, stop the bleeding. I walked one block, then another, careful to step over the upturned pavers, the uneven tiles, the holes left behind. Whole streets are under construction all over this city.

Maybe there would be a real restaurant with water, and I could stop and clean myself. But nothing. "How far is the pharmacy?" I asked a passerby. "Over there," he pointed.

I walked one more block; it was getting late. Finally, I found it, just behind a pole that seemed to stand guard in front of its door. The pharmacy was really just a counter at street level, like a fast-food counter, except the shelves had medical boxes instead of bread or condiments. Part of a chain called Similarity, it didn't inspire confidence, but I was relieved. Here I could find help.

When I showed my elbow to the guy behind the counter, in the belief that he was the pharmacist, he moved his head no. "Go to a doctor."

"What? This is a pharmacy." I'm usually a nice person, but I think I was pretty rude. I must have yelled. We're all so spoiled in the States. "You should have something to clean, help with this." I said in Spanish, hoping to elicit more cooperation.

"We can't do that. Only a doctor."

"Ok, just help me as a human being then," I said. "I need alcohol, cotton, Band-Aids. You should have that."

Something must have clicked inside his brain. He looked around and came back with a large plastic bag full of stuff. It read "Botiquin Kit" on the outside. "This has everything," he said.

"I only need alcohol and cotton to clean the wound."

"This has it." He kept the bag in his hand.

"OK, how much is it?"

Slowly he scanned the bag. My elbow kept bleeding. I glared at him, but I got no reaction.

"166 pesos," he finally said. I made a mental calculation and figured that eight dollars was worth it to avoid an infection that would ruin the rest of my stay in this city. Did I say I love San Miguel de Allende? "OK."

It took several further glares and a request for help — "Me ayuda por favor?" — for this person to open the bag and take out some of the stuff inside. He wore a white medical uniform, but he was just a simple clerk, a salesman of whatever was on the pharmacy shelves. He first took out a couple of small bottles with names I didn't recognize. Violeta de genciana, mertodol tintura.

"Alcohol?" I said and he dug inside the bag once more and came up with a larger white bottle and a smaller plastic bag. It took a few more of my not friendly looks for him to find the cotton and open the alcohol bottle.

When he saw me cringe as I cleaned the dirt from the mess on my elbow, he left and came back with a box marked "botiquin." It was a type of first aid kit, smaller than the plastic bag with the same name. "This should heal the wound," he said and opened the box. It contained different sizes of dressings, rolled bandages and a couple of bottles with unknown liquid.

"I need Band-Aids, the kit should have them, right?" I said, although I hadn't seen any inside the kit.

In silence, he dug around the box and pulled a piece of gauze out of a paper envelope and paper tape. He might have been right. The elbow needed more than a couple of band aids. When I left, the kit was inside my backpack, the elbow half covered with gauze and tape, a piece of alcohol wet cotton was on my left hand to stop the bleeding. There were no band-aids inside the first aid kit.

While I walked back, I reflected on the experience. My impatience with inefficiency and my lack of empathy when I saw incompetence. Could I have acted in a different way to obtain a different result? I didn't have an answer, but I wasn't proud of myself.

There is a poignant ending to this story. I got to the theater in time. My friend had reserved a seat and I had some time left before the performances started. There was a new café on the corner, less than half a block from the theater, and I was starving. When I entered to get a small bite to eat, the owner was more than solicitous. She offered me the bathroom so I could wash away the dirt, and Band-Aids. The food came quickly and was delicious. I felt her kindness and was grateful.

The guy in charge of the open mic, someone who said his name was Shane, put my reading as number 10, so I'd have an hour to wait until my turn. Enough to observe the entertainment or mull and fret over my fall. I did both. Most of the *performers were musicians and male. Only one other writer, and he was a comedian, and only one other woman, a country singer with her guitarist partner. I wondered if I was out of place here.*

While I listened to the music, some of it quite good and some horrible, I reflected on the neighborhood I had accidentally stepped into, rather than on my tendency to fall. A place where there were almost no pharmacies, few stores and only small dingy eateries that lacked running water.

As to falling, I had fallen twice, six months before, while visiting my son in Austin. Both times on the same day, tripping on uneven streets and with my dog on a leash. The combination of bumpy streets, dog and the type of sandals I was wearing, with too much space between my toes and the end of the sandal, had been how I had rationalized the falls. Since then, I had bought shorter sandals that I thought were just right for my feet, and there was no dog. And yet, I had fallen again. Worse: all of these falls were equally graceless and undignified. The top of my foot caught a lip of the pavement and my whole body went down like a wooden pole, no bending, no turning, just my hands out, with an iPhone in one of them. Yes. I found the cause: distraction, lack of focus. Because I believe I'm not uncoordinated. After all, I dance Zumba and do yoga almost every day, and I've practiced balance since I turned sixty. I can stand on one leg for 10 minutes. But it's my brain that lacks balance or presence. It has its own time and space, makes up stories or plans the future as I walk, careless of what is in front of my feet.

I did read two of my short prose pieces and a poem, glad to rise to the challenge. I embraced the applause I got after each of them. Any mishap is a learning opportunity. What did I get out of all this? Here is a list:

1. *I love San Miguel de Allende. I always thought it was a magical city full of music and bright colors.*

But part of that is an illusion we conjure when we live in the world as tourists or well-to-do foreigners. There is another side where there is still music, but the colors are drab, and poverty cancels the allure.

2. *My brain needs to focus on the moment, avoid distractions, live in the present. Yes, I know, this is trite, but worth remembering.*

3. *I'm lucky, but how many more lucky turns will I have?*

4. *And the final cliché. I got this from Shane at the theater: I am one more of the fallen women of San Miguel. Or as we say in Argentina when we fall on the pavement: I bought the city. Now it belongs to me, and I don't have to pay taxes.*

I was conjuring this story, these images as I sat at the edge of my cot, in this small hotel with "sin" in its name. I sat there, and I wrote about the day in my journal while I caressed the bruise on my cheek, checked again my scrapes. I thought that here I was, thousands of miles away from San Miguel, in time and space, but I haven't learned lesson number two yet, and I need to stop buying — with my bodily injuries — all the places I love.

Forgiveness

Molinaseca to Villafranca del Bierzo, Spain

May 4, 2019

Gargoyles of the soil

Pardoned

Today, at 9 a.m., after breakfast, we said our goodbyes to the cute guy, the manager of the hotel, left our rooms and our sins at Josanas's in Molinaseca, and set out on the next leg of our hike. My cheek looked better under a lot of make-up, and I decorated my chin with a couple of nice band-aids. It was already starting to scar. My body felt fine, I wasn't even tired. I'd slept like a log the whole night. Am I strong or lucky? "Maybe it's all that coffee, or the yogurt with cereal you like so much," was Nelly's comment. Better I don't say anything or ask why she made that comment. Don't be sarcastic, I tell myself, enjoy the ride. And yet, those observations annoy me and I don't know how to respond to them.

We expected an easy day, the altitude map showed no steep ups or downs. However, when we arrived at our next stop, a hostel in Villafranca del Bierzo, it was already past 8 p.m. The late evening summer sunset illuminated the blue and cream façade of the place where we planned to stay for two nights.

Margaret and I, we are always the last to arrive at the hotels for the night. We like to look around, stop for coffee and many bathroom breaks, I take pictures. But today, I believe we just walked for most of the 11.5 hours. Most of the morning we walked together. Sometimes chatting, sometimes in silence. Our conversations are not deep, we need our energy to keep the pace. I'm also somewhat dumbstruck by my surroundings.

"When are you planning to retire?" I ask Nelly to break one of the silences, although I think she already said that she had to wait for her current project to be completed. She is the only one of us still working full time. "Probably in a year or two," she says. Then we talk about our hobbies and I mention again that I enjoy working with beads. She describes the bags of beads she inherited from her dead sister. "I would love to look at them," I say. We do not discuss the dead, we keep talking about the beauty of different beads.

When it gets to be lunch time, we find a place to eat and the four of us sit together. Lunch is a sacred stop during these long hikes and we discuss the lunch options. I have one of those wonderful Spanish omelets, made with three of those tasty, orange-colored fresh eggs, mushrooms, and onions. The eggs are orange not because they are super fresh, gathered in the morning from the hens nearby, but because those hens are pasture raised, foraging on green plants and bugs, fed vegetables like carrots, sweet potatoes, chard or kale. Not a mix of grain feed, vitamins and minerals, as in most of the U.S.

We can only take an hour to enjoy the lunch, but if I were by myself, I would have taken most of the afternoon. I not only like to eat, but I find joy in watching the people go by, listening in on their conversations and dreaming. So maybe it is a good thing that I am with three other companions who are more task-oriented and understand time better than I do.

As the afternoon wears on, we start to separate into pairs. Margaret and I take more short breaks than the N's and walk at an easier pace. Even with the many breaks, the stretch at the end of the day is long and seems to last forever. For the final two hours, there's no sign of other humans, just fields: tilled fields, blooming fields, wheat, chard, lettuce and those cut up trunks of the grape vines that to me look like gargoyles of the soil, their grotesque shapes waiting to be transformed, waiting to bloom. Some gargoyles have the bride-green crowns of initial bloom. These grape vine trunks, stocky, woodsy, twisted, mutate their ugliness into beauty and sweetness when they are crowned.

The grapevines remind me of Quasimodo and Paris, Notre Dame. My mind starts to figure out the logistics for the trip to Paris that I have planned two weeks after I get back from this pilgrimage. It's not easy, but I tell my brain to stop, focus on the present, the adventure I'm living right now, rather than the one I will live in the future.

As we get closer to the finish line, the landscape looks more and more like a land of dreams. Gentle hills covered with rows and rows of recently planted vegetables and the gargoyle or crowned grape vines. A golden green and brown illuminated by the rays of a sun sitting low in the sky. In the background, the large gray and purple mountains, and every so often on top of a hill, a small white farmhouse or a little church, letting us know that there are people somewhere around, even if we haven't seen anybody along our way. I keep taking pictures so we'll remember the beauty because, at the moment, as much as I try, I can't quite appreciate it. My feet are sore after walking 30 kilometers. At the point where the map shows the town should be, we can see it, but from a cliff above, and we fret about how much longer it will take us to get down.

A Fairytale Ending

No spiritual revelations yet,
just endurance during an 11-hour walk
with very few breaks.

Cliffs and trees.
Few signs,
no people —
We wonder
Is this the right path?

I remember yesterday's promise:
I'm protected,
I say to myself,
my mouth in a smirk.
And I am.

After many hours,
a glance from above
of a few roofs
between the green canopies.
We hear music,
echoing up the hill,
from the town below.

It takes another half hour,
maybe more,
to walk all the way down

and find
our hotel.
The sign at the front
reads:
"Puerta del Perdón"
the Gate to Forgiveness.
Pale blue,
like the one in the picture books
I read as a child.

Forgive Our Sins

The path down from the cliff seemed like a spiral that encircled the village below at its center. This shape allowed us to hear music and voices coming from the town's houses and streets as we descended.

"We're there," I said, and on my tired legs I did a little jig of joy, not knowing that it would take us another hour to make it to the town gate and reach the hostel.

When we finally got there, the name above the hostel entrance door read *Puerta del Perdón* (Gate to Forgiveness). The door was pale blue and there was a golden halo around it from the last rays of the setting sun. I felt hope and purpose, as if this could be a gate into a new dimension in my life. Maybe this was a bit of spirituality inching stealthily inside my brain, which tends to dismiss the unproved intangible. Although I do admire the harmony of nature, the sights that offer peace to the soul, there is a continuous struggle, a tension between my intellect and my emotions. But I don't fight against that tension; I like that part of myself. I don't like to admit that as a child, I learned to put boundaries around my emotions. Since my mother died, I have built fences, closed the gates to intense feelings to avoid pain. Maybe I need this trip to learn how to open those gates.

At the sight of the sign above the door, Margaret and I laughed and started to discuss whether we might need forgiveness.

"Maybe for our ambition to complete this walk?" she said.

"What is a sin? Is ambition a sin?" I asked. I don't believe in a God or a religion; I believe that it is a sin to behave in a way that hurts your fellow human beings. I think that ambition is not wrong; the desire for excellence, to strive for the next goal post, should be applauded. Without it, the human race might stagnate. But then, the unbounded pursuit of glory can lead us to be cruel to our fellow humans. That, in my book, would be a sin. And sometimes we don't realize that, as we go towards our next goal post, we are unkind, or just plain mean. Or maybe this is just a criticism meant mostly for myself.

I said to Margaret, tongue in cheek, "Just in case, it would be nice if we could find compassion or exoneration here. After all, we left our sins in Molinaseca." The name of our previous hotel (Josana's Sin) had been the source of some facetious teasing and discussion about sin — mainly associated with our reflections about the clerk of that hotel, who was young and handsome.

Margaret is OK with my irreligious comments. I try to keep them from coming out when Nellie and Nelly are around. I believe, though I don't know for sure, that they might be offended. I know that it is part of my makeup to try to avoid unnecessary confrontation. Then I wonder why expressing my thoughts or my feelings about sins or exoneration would offend anybody. But that's a discussion with myself that I don't want to have, not yet.

We Find a Friend

The town of Villafranca del Bierzo has castles, and the cobble-stone streets are narrow. They go up and down, become alleys, and then turn around, inviting walkers to get lost between medieval views. The outside of the hostel is light blue, like those in children's tales, and when Margaret and I get there, we hear a noise from one of the windows. Nellie and Nelly (who arrived at least half an hour ago) are tapping on the glass and waving at us. They seem excited. Once inside, we find them sitting at one of the small hostel dining tables with a man. They introduce him as Daniel. He is a small guy, probably in his mid-sixties, balding, wearing eyeglasses, and he has a kind smile. Nellie and Nelly look rested and happy, they're laughing and flirting with this man. I think they were missing someone new and male to chat with, but it turns out that this man is also quite interesting to talk with. Daniel has been hiking El Camino all the way from where it starts at Saint-Jean-Pied-de-Port on the French side of the Pyrenees. He's already walked four weeks longer than we have, through snow and rain, but he looks as if he just started out. Maybe the difference is that he has been hiking, taking serious hikes, all his life.

Margaret and I sit at a table next to the N's and Daniel because the hostel tables only sit four and they're already finishing dinner. The smell of food and the bright tablecloths, the view of the town castle from the window, give us a second wind. We try to chat from table to table and get up to speed with Daniel's story, but the N's keep asking him questions and interjecting exclamations of surprise and awe. Eventually we learn that Daniel used to hike with his wife, whom he lost last year. He promised her that he would continue hiking after her death.

His last hike was in Japan and he shows the N's, and then us, some of the pictures he took on that journey. He opens the notebook where he writes about his day to also show us some of the pictures from the current hike that he has pasted there. We marvel at his story and are in awe of his journal that is a work of art. He takes pictures and prints them with a portable printer he carries with him. Then, he glues them into his journal. His handwriting is a perfect and even cursive in blue ink, and he doesn't seem to make mistakes. There are no strikeouts, or scratches on his pages. Afterwards, the N's who like to flirt, tease me about this guy. "He is single, available and likes to travel," they say. Yes, he is nice and kind, but I have no interest. I am curious, however, about his approach to keep the sorrow for the dead at bay.

The hostel manager is kind, notices how tired we are, and hurries to serve us a meal that she's cooked herself, then she gives us information about the town. We will stay here another day and night. It is our rest day, and an opportunity to finally have a place and time to do laundry, make a new friend. From when we started to when we finish in Santiago, we'll have just two of these rest days, so we have to make the best of them — especially this pause, this break before we launch on the next stretch, advertised as one of the hardest of this hike.

We Rest

Villafranca del Bierzo, Spain

May 5, 2019

Welcome to a day of rest

A Pause on the Way

Today is Sunday, rest day in Villafranca de Bierzo, a quaint town with a medieval castle hidden under a cliff. At the *Puerta del Perdón* hostel, where we're staying, we are pampered by Estela, the manager, a woman in her early forties, of medium build, with dark short curly hair and a ready smile, who takes care of the eight rooms spread over two floors with the help of one part-time assistant. She doesn't seem to ever stop, but she does not appear hassled either. When we first arrived, she had a delicious, home-cooked dinner waiting for us, and this morning, the breakfast included a homemade cake, fresh squeezed juice and the perfect coffee. When we mention laundry, she offers to do it for us; she will tend the clothes in the sun, and everything will be ready, sweet smelling and folded by the evening.

At the breakfast table by the window, with the sun reflecting off the small vase that holds little cornflowers and the morning view of the round stone tower of the town castle, we read our guide for the next day. We imagine that tomorrow will be our hardest day yet. But we are at *La Puerta del Perdón*, so we'll be forgiven for our arrogance, our wish to do something challenging, as if we were young again.

Estela hears our chat and comes down with more orange juice, jam and toast to calm our anxiety. "Piece of cake," she says. "You walk to Herrería, have lunch there and then, boom, go up all the way to the top and you're in O'Cerbreiro. You'll be there before evening." When we look at her with doubt in our eyes, she says, "I did it twice. After the second time, I decided to stay in this town." But we know better. We have read the guide, and looked at the kilometers, and the slope going up.

However, today will be a day of repose, a break, we'll figure out tonight how to manage the rest. Thus, we've started with this breakfast at 9 a.m. instead of 8 a.m., and we've taken our time. We don't have to hike anywhere today. Margaret and I make plans. We'd like to visit the town, but Nellie and Nelly are fired up. Nelly wants to go to church, she wants to hear mass. "It doesn't start until 12 p.m.," I say, "This is Spain." But no way. They go out while Margaret and I enjoy our fruit, tarts, goat cheese and the pampering of Estela, who keeps offering us more coffee, more cake, a piece of fresh bread, marmalade. "Rest, rest," she says. It must show in our faces, even if I don't feel it, how tired we are.

It's amazing to watch these two women taking care of the eight rooms, changing beds and towels, cooking, cleaning, taking care of the needs of all the peregrines at the hostel. We give them our clothes to wash. They will be dried on clotheslines, in the sun. No automatic drying machines here. I'm not even sure they have a washing machine. They have eight rooms in total, but we have only met Daniel and a young couple so far. As some pilgrims leave early in the morning, new pilgrims will be arriving in the afternoon.

When Margaret and I finish stuffing our stomachs with food, we attack our emails and I stuff myself on Facebook and social media, but the sun is shining, and my curiosity about the town wins over my addiction to the screen. Margaret and I decide to walk toward the center of town, and as we open the door of the hostel, we meet Nellie and Nelly, who are back, and, as predicted, didn't find any mass. "They don't have anything until noon," Nelly complains.

The four of us set out together for a walk to the town center, about a mile away, and of course, most of it uphill. We find people milling around, it's a holiday. Some women are wearing summer dresses and the men long khaki pants instead of jeans; they will be going to church. It's easy to distinguish the town folk from the hikers, with their boots and shorts, backpacks and hats. And yet, in this town of hikers and working-class people, Nelly looks to me as if she's dressed for a walk in Milan. I know that this thought is unkind, but she's wearing a long black skirt and carrying a large yellow purse. The only casual thing she wears are flip flops on her feet. Her feet are sore, with the beginnings of blisters, not good. After a stroll, Nellie and Nelly are done and go back to the hotel. Margaret and I, we are fearless. We continue, have a coffee, take selfies at a table on the plaza, under the sun, buy stuff to make sandwiches, and I find polvorones, a type of cookie I used to eat when I was a child in Buenos Aires. This kind of cookie is not known, or not well known, in the U.S..

Afterwards, we look for a pharmacy where we can get sunscreen and Band-Aids. Margaret is also beginning to have issues with her feet. Most pharmacies are closed today, but eventually we succeed in finding one that's open. It is still early afternoon, and we don't feel like we're done with the town yet. We end up walking up and down the cobblestone paths. We find a cliff and stairs, and a church that was under construction for 200 years, between 1600 and 1800. The church should have been larger, but there was no money. In the end, it feels like another hike, just an easier one. We seem to have fallen into this walking/hiking habit by now. Our Fitbits show that today we have done more than 20,000 steps, just 10 miles, piece of cake.

At day's end, we meet again, the four of us, for an early dinner at a restaurant recommended by our manager, Estela. We need to make it back to the hostel early and fall asleep fast. We devise a strategy for tomorrow: Nelly and I will walk up to O'Cerbreiro, a long, long 32-kilometer walk with a steep ascent in the last 12 kilometers, while Margaret and Nellie plan to take a taxi to Herrería, the stop before the climb, and just hike from there. They are afraid of this long walk, although Estela has insisted, "It will be child's play."

The plan for Nelly and I is to leave at 7:30 a.m. and have breakfast on the way. It will be hard for me. I'll need to get up at 6:30 a.m. to have the bag and the backpack ready. And yet, Estela, the hostel manager/server/jack of all trades, insists, when we get back from dinner, that she will leave a tray with coffee and packed breakfast at our door, so we can have something before we start.

Before I go to sleep, I fuss around with my bag and lighten the backpack, so it will be easier to carry on the way up. What I take from the backpack has to fit inside my carry-on bag —not an easy feat, since the bag is pretty full already. There go the rain pants and some of the old snacks, and one of the extra layers. But I still need to take my jacket, and lots of water, even if I don't drink that much, and the emergency kit, and the flashlight, and the portable charger for the phone. In the end, this thing still must weigh close to 10 pounds. I can't get rid of the what-ifs. What if I get lost, or if I need help, or if I fall again and I'm alone, or if gets very cold, or if...? Infinite ifs inside my head. It is later than I'd planned when I finally put my head on the pillow and close my eyes. The images of trees, cobblestones, cliffs and steep hills turn around in circles inside my brain.

Lighten the Load

*Villafranca del Bierzo
to O'Cebreiro, Spain
May 6, 2019*

Entrance to Herreria. Stone reads, "stop, breathe, observe."

An Early Start

A big, long day ahead of us, at least for the two of us who start at dawn. The two who don't quite see eye-to-eye, even if it doesn't show. We are friendly, and care about each other's well-being, but I feel an undercurrent of hostility. Or maybe it's the grating comments, comments that might not be, but sound, at least to me, judgmental. Like, "How many coffees did you have?" — the implication being that I drink too many in the morning. Or, "I like eggs for breakfast, but this is OK," referring to the typical Spanish tortilla, a concoction of eggs and potatoes that people usually eat at noon or later but that can be available in the morning. The Spanish hotels don't always have scrambled or over-easy eggs for breakfast. And although the words do not say so, exactly, it sounds, even if it's not meant to be, like a critique of all of us who do not eat eggs in the morning. I eat yogurt and fruit. I keep my mouth shut, which is difficult. Later I'll learn that Margaret has also noticed Nelly's habit of making what sound like negative or judgmental comments. But it could just be a personality trait. Or maybe Margaret and I are being too sensitive, reading too much into her words.

Still, we two, Nelly and me, are the ones with enough motivation and energy to do the 32-kilometer walk today. Me, because I think it will be enjoyable to see the unknown landscape, take on a new challenge, and of course, because I'm somewhat competitive and stubborn. I believe that my friend Nelly is just as competitive and stubborn, but I also think that she is so focused on the end result that, most of the time, she doesn't enjoy the journey. For some reason, that bothers me.

It's possible that I am irritated because I want to explore, find joy in the experience itself, but I know that sometimes I can act in the same way she does. We tend to be annoyed by traits that we don't like but that are too close to those we have in ourselves.

The breakfast tray that the hostel manager left at my door has a thermos of coffee, a hard-boiled egg, a sandwich, cereal, yogurt, a slice of cake. I open the thermos and notice that the coffee has milk; I drink it black. I put some of the food into my backpack and go downstairs. It is exactly 7:30 a.m., an ungodly hour for me to be ready. I've been a night owl since birth, so I'm proud of myself for being on time.

My friend is already at the door. "I slept with my clothes on," she says, and although I know she probably doesn't mean it in that way, her words sound critical, as if that is what one is supposed to do to be on time for an early morning start. As if I'm already late. Am I becoming a grouchy old woman?

And here we go. A beautiful morning, a joyful first few kilometers, over a bridge crossing one of the many rivers along the route. We take a selfie and then a passerby takes our picture, in front of a river, a sunrise — pink, blue and white sky. We smile. We stop for a quick breakfast at a café where we also eat some of the stuff from our backpacks; a bathroom break, and then we are outside the city gates. We're euphoric about the adventure ahead.

How We Get to Herrería

Herrería, the stop before the climb and where we plan to have lunch, is about 20 kilometers away. Although the path is smooth, the walk is long, and we don't want to stop. The recommended plan is to be ready to ascend by 2 p.m., to ensure that we won't have to hurry to make it to the top for dinner while it's still light.

The path is part concrete, part gravel, part plain dirt, all of it winding through a wondrous landscape, between tall trees and a forest with all sorts of green. The singing of the birds accompanies us. I stop and take a picture when I notice my friend is lagging behind, her walk unsteady, her face pale. Her feet, which have been getting worse as we walk, now hurt too much. She still pushes herself with a focused mind, but at some point, she thinks she might faint, she wants to give up. We rest at the side of the road. I suggest she loosen her boots, maybe they are tied too tightly. That helps for a while, but our pace is slow.

She says, "Go ahead, I'll call for a taxi." But I know better than to leave her stranded before we make it to town. That's why we walk in pairs, to take care of each other. I cajole, we stop, we talk, I give her energy gummies. It feels like a miracle when we arrive in Herrería. At the entrance to the town, there is a small stream, pink ribbons around the trees and a big rock that reads *"Parar, Respirar, Observar"* (Stop, Breathe, Observe) — and we do, before we go for another 100 meters and stop at the café. We order lunch. I take off my boots, massage my feet, convince her to do the same.

Progress

"I'll take a taxi from here," she says, after we've recovered a bit. We ask the waiter, who seems to be also the owner of the café, about the price for a taxi and how long it would take to pick her up. When he says 20 euros, and maybe half an hour to get there, we think that the price is a bit exorbitant, and it would take too long. Nelly wavers, but she thinks she can't go on. There is another guy sitting next to us who says he's sick and he could share a taxi. That seems to brighten Nelly up, although I'm not sure it's a great idea to share a taxi with a stranger who is sick. But I keep silent. We'll see.

An hour goes by, we have a good lunch. I suggest to Nelly that maybe she can make it to the top if we go slowly, rest in between. I know that it would be a pity to have gotten here and miss the best part. The views on this next stretch of the Camino are advertised as fantastic. I also know that Nelly will be very unhappy if she doesn't go on; she can't bear the idea of quitting against a challenge. Her feet are betraying her will.

Indeed, after food and rest, Nelly feels better. She changes her mind, she will try to make it on foot as far as she can. I think, but I don't say, that once we start up, there is no way back, no way to get a taxi. The map doesn't show any roads, only the path and only one rest stop on the way up.

The sick guy decides to walk with us when we leave the cafe. As soon as we begin to climb, we are rewarded with the sight of an awe-inspiring landscape. Layers upon layers of rolling hills covered with light and dark grasses, surrounded by white flowering bushes, sprinkled all over with yellow wildflowers and, in the far background, wondrous purple mountains, a few small farmhouses, and a blue sky full of white clouds. The higher we go, the larger the number of hills we can see, the more changing patterns of green, yellow and purple hues as the path becomes steeper and more difficult to navigate. And yet, my whole body smiles, nothing hurts.

Little by little we make progress. There is a bench on the way, and we rest while Nelly eats the snacks from her backpack. She carries a whole lunch and dinner inside that backpack. Where I lighten my load, she seems to weigh hers down with food for the road. The sick guy sits on the bench next to us. Then, he gets up, he looks recovered and walks ahead, surprisingly fast. "He doesn't seem to be that sick after all," Nelly says as she stands.

View on the way to O'Cerbreiro

Uphill to the End

After a few more hours of walking, I suggest we stop at a cafe where we can sit on a chair and be served. I crave coffee. "You go. I'll eat from my backpack here. We shouldn't dillydally," Nelly says as she leans against a ledge by the path. I guess ours is the difference between looking at this as a journey to enjoy or believing this is a challenge that must be conquered, that only the end matters. I look at her face and I don't insist. However, an hour later, about two thirds of the way to the top, I demand that we sit at a café and have something to eat. We must have a proper rest.

I want to make sure both of us make it in one piece to the end. There are no cabs around here if she faints. "If you want to eat from your backpack, that's fine, but we have to stop and sit. I want to be pampered before the final push," I say. Her face is pale, and she walks with effort. I know that her feet are not well, but I don't say so. They must be covered with blisters and must hurt like crazy; her boots are too small. I feel for her.

It turns out to be a smart move. The place where we stop, my friend under duress, is sunny and full of young people laughing and drinking beer. We can see the green and purple fields below; this is a lookout, we're quite high. I take pictures of the scenery and of the young people who giggle and make a racket next to us.

A few of the girls are in sandals, flip flops, due to the blisters on their feet. "Do you hike in those?" my friend asks, and when they smile and say yes, she also smiles. "Tomorrow, I hike in my flip flops," she says. But these women are more than forty years younger than we are, you can twist an ankle that way, I think, but I don't say it out loud.

While we sit, I look out in a state of bliss and wait to be served, my friend digs inside her backpack. And then we hear bells and barking, and soon, passing right next to our table through the narrow street, a parade of cows, calves and a bull coming back from the pastures below, accompanied by a pack of dogs. The cows are smooth, light brown, the dogs are black and brown and white. A mixed breed of cattle dogs, their ears up, focused on their herding job. One in front, many at the back. The animals and their herdsmen pass so close that we can touch them. We all take pictures, a video, joy, it's a feast. We close our eyes to keep the memory alive.

When the parade is over, we have to go. We have to make it the rest of the way up before it is too late and we lose the light, or we are so tired that we make a mistake. We start the final climb. Up we go, Nelly conquers pain and I conquer doubt. And the view is so astounding that it justifies all the steps it's taken to get there. The trail rises and dips between hills carpeted in all hues of green and purple, brown, yellow and white, the dark green and gray mountains behind, a canyon, a valley looking down, a clear white and blue sky. We cross paths with a young group and we raise and click our iPhones. "Where are you from?" "Germany, Norway." Tough gals with tape on their ankles

At the very end there is a statue of a young woman, sitting on the wall overlooking the valley below. The copper she is made of has turned green; her calm face welcomes us to the village of O'Cerbreiro. We raise our arms in victory.

However, as usual, to enter the village proper and get to the hotel, there are still more steps. Soon, we see a building with a thatched roof, a guy walking without a backpack and, after a few more turns, we find the building and the entrance to the hotel. And it's not even 7 p.m. Our bags are waiting at the entrance and we are ready to rest, take a shower, eat. But on our way to our rooms, the other two friends, who arrived earlier, come out and scream, "Welcome, you made it!" This is followed by, "There is a mass at 7:30 p.m. for the Santiago pilgrims! You can make it if you hurry."

Seven Days

After only six days
I have conquered fear,
carry less physical and mental weight,
have made a promise
(to be a gentler, kinder self).

After 32 kilometers, 13 of them uphill,
the legs hurt,
the feet hurt,
the back hurts.
And yet, the heart is content,
adrenaline runs high.

Still no spiritual revelations.
I work to lighten my load instead.
Leave unwanted weight behind.
Leave fear, leave envy, leave guilt,
leave all the "have-tos" in my head,
the need for extra tasks.

I won't let go of the memories
and the grief of so many losses
of so many deaths, is still stuck
in a side pocket of my brain.
And yet I eat with gusto,
I sleep well.

After all, in only six days
I have conquered fear,
carry less weight,
have made a promise
(to be a gentler, kinder self).
And on the seventh day,
I will rest.

Victorious entrance to O'Cerbreiro

A Peregrine Mass

I have doubts about going to mass. Why do I care about a mass when, after all, I am a secular Jew? But my tired friend, the one with the blisters who could barely make the last kilometer, gets a second wind, jumps up. "I'll be there in 10 minutes," she says. And me? I can't miss an opportunity. What if it's something special? So, I also shower in 10 minutes, a record for me, and then I am ready to walk to the small church to observe the mass.

"I don't plan to stay long," I say to Margaret, "I just want to see the church and take a few pictures." Margaret, who is agnostic but grew up Catholic, tells me not to worry, it will probably be an abbreviated mass since all pilgrims are exhausted and want to eat. She explains mass to me along the way. There will be an opening prayer, some readings and liturgy, and a communion rite.

The other two friends are super excited, they rush to the church. Daniel is also there, the guy we met at the Villa Franca stop. He's going to translate the mass from Spanish into English from the pulpit.

Although I'm a secular Jew, an atheist at heart, with a scientific mind, sitting between Catholic pilgrims, I'm affected by the whole ceremony. My previous mass experiences have only happened when my husband and I accidentally caught an occasional mass during visits to cathedrals in Europe. We loved the architecture of the old buildings, and we would stare at their baroque or rococo adornments, but we'd usually just stay inside for a few minutes to enjoy the choir and take pictures. This is different.

The O'Cerbreiro church is warm, stark white and gray. I appreciate the lack of a Jesus dripping blood and almost no saintly figures adorning the walls. The priest is young, dressed in a simple gold embroidered robe, and he tries his best to be inclusive. As part of the mass, he provides translations in French, English, Italian and Portuguese that are read by one of those fluent in the language. There are no French pilgrims, but there is a Canadian from Montreal who speaks French. A Brazilian reads the Portuguese version. Nellie and Nelly read parts of the English version, but it is Daniel who reads the longer part at the beginning. I think that Nelly has forgotten her pain in the bliss of being part of this mass. Although my smile is a performance of my soul, my face a lie, I feel the emotion of connection when, at the end of the mass, the priest embraces each of us: twelve or thirteen pilgrims, four or five languages between us. When he gives me a little stone with a yellow arrow to guard me during the rest of El Camino, I put it in my pocket and, later, inside my backpack. I'll carry it with me to the end of this journey. Is this the way I have lightened my load, by embracing others, or have I just weighed myself down with a false belief?

I'm starved and almost fainting when we get to the restaurant. But this is a very small city, just a few houses, a hotel, maybe two. There is a single restaurant, that is also a café, and the food is not great, but we drink a beer, and all is well.

*Mass at O'Cerbreiro (Daniel sitting against the wall
as we wait for the priest)*

Outsider – 1958

I'm kneeling on the dirty concrete floor, next to a cane chair. The palms of my hands touch each other, and my arms lean on prickly interlaced strips of rattan. "Bow your head," the teacher says, but my neck doesn't bend, my eyes are fixed on the colorful drawings hanging on the wall. It is religion class — and this is the first image that appears in my mind when anyone asks me what it was like to grow up Jewish in Buenos Aires, Argentina.

Today, that memory seems quaint or surreal. So much so, that not long ago, I asked an Argentinean friend of mine if I wasn't making it up. I wasn't, although I had managed to distort the memory so that it no longer hurt.

From kindergarten until fifth grade, I had the usual language, math and science classes. Once a week we had drawing, music, PE and religion — Catholic religion, the official religion of the country. And every year, at the beginning of the school year, the teacher would ask who had to leave the room during religion class, who was not Catholic, and I had to raise my hand. Would they know if I didn't? It wouldn't be obvious from my last name, or my facial features. I can pass for someone with German or Swedish ancestry. But of course, my parents had already informed the school. I couldn't hide.

"Nemirovsky and Zales, go to the patio," the teacher would say at the beginning of the class, and the two of us, the outcasts, the Jews (there were no other religions and no atheists in that class) would go out to the yard, a large square made of gray and cracked stone blocks. Rain or shine, cold or hot, we went out. Once in a while, the principal, crossing the yard,

would see us jumping around to stay warm and let us inside to do homework in her office. It was always just the two of us.

So why was I in class that day, learning to pray with a chair? It was first grade and Nemirovsky was absent. The teacher said it would be good for me to learn about religion, Catholic religion. The whole lesson must have been so foreign and intense that the image has stuck inside my head to be retrieved still intact almost sixty years later.

I didn't like my classmate Nemirovsky — we didn't use first names and I don't know what her first name was. She was tall, with a long face, a large nose and a name that couldn't hide its origin. She was proud of who she was. I wasn't like her, and I wasn't proud of my Jewishness.

My parents, both born and raised in Argentina, weren't religious. My father, a socialist, was quite secular, and we went to temple only on the High Holy days, as a social event. However, my parents spoke Yiddish if they didn't want me to know what they were talking about, and we followed Jewish behaviors. One of them being a limited interaction with the outside world, the "others," because there was only safety and security among those "like us." At each new encounter, there was always the question: Is he or she from the "colectividad?" A term that was, and still is, only used to denote being part of the Jewish community. Family, close connections were the "mishpokhe." Our tribe. Anybody else was catalogued as a "goy" or a "shikse."

Thus, my home life centered on family and close friends. I don't remember that I ever invited a school classmate home, and I don't remember being invited to a classmate's home until I was eleven years old.

At school, I tried my hardest to pass; I wanted to be the same as everyone else. It was difficult, when they talked about Jesus and compared little stamps of saints or brought chocolate eggs during Easter. Those customs were foreign to me, but I would smile, nod my head and keep my mouth shut. Sometimes, walking back from school, I would enter one of the big

Catholic churches. They were so much nicer and so much more imposing than our plain synagogue!

I believed that I could be like everyone else, fit in, if I just didn't call attention to who I was, if I hid my secret. I nodded understanding when I heard the kids talk about mass, communion or confirmation. But of course, I didn't understand.

Most of the time, I could almost be one of them. Then, without warning or cause, a kid would run up to me and yell, "You killed Jesus," and I was so taken aback that I didn't know what else to answer other than, "No, I didn't."

And then, after religion class, some of our classmates would come to us alone in the schoolyard and ask, "Do you drink the blood of little babies?" I would try to remain invisible, but Nemirovsky would answer back. "No, we don't, where did you get that from?" The kid might answer back with a slur and, sometimes, the back and forth would escalate to a fight requiring teacher intervention. I didn't like Nemirovsky then, but today I am glad she was there. The lies and the insults of that time still burn and sting, many years later, under all my fluffy pillows of carefully crafted denial.

Before I turned twelve years old, we moved to another neighborhood. There was a change of official policy, and no more religion classes. I could finally hide myself from myself. If I was not branded, I thought I would be safe. The damage that this can do to a growing brain is the source of a whole different book.

Funny, I think, as I look back: I had forgotten these stories. I am still not religious, I could never figure out how one God, if it existed, could be better than another one, and how many single Gods could exist. I don't identify as a religious Jew, but I am proud of my ancestry.

I married a Catholic, a very lapsed one, but still one who was baptized, had his confirmation or communion, and even assisted the priest when he was very young. My sons have grown up not just non-religious, but nearly anti-religious, although our family delights in the celebration of all holidays.

When my husband died, we organized a Pastafarian memorial. Google what this means. I cooked pasta and salsa for sixty people. During those first two weeks, that celebration, and all the friends who came to our made-up memorial, saved and helped us more than any praying could have done.

PART II

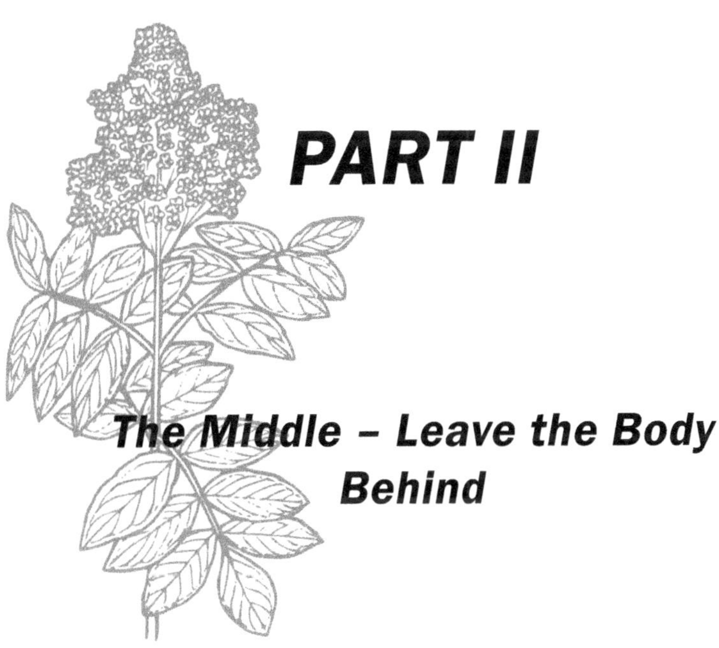

The Middle – Leave the Body Behind

Look Within

O'Cebreiro to Samos, via Triacastela, Spain

May 7, 2019

Hike our way up

1st Stage: O'Cebreiro to Triacastela

The next day, in O'Cebreiro, we decide to shop after breakfast and before we start our walk. There is a single store that sells everything you might need when you hike. We have now entered Galicia, this is "Celt country" in Spain. The etched patterns in the jewelry are the same as I saw in Ireland last year. We buy tchotchkes, a bracelet, El Camino socks, a bottle opener and Nelly, who has the worst blisters, buys a pair of shoes that look more like clogs than athletic shoes. She's convinced that they will be perfect because they don't hurt her feet; the rest of us know they are just "after-the-hike" shoes, but we don't say it. I guess because Nelly likes her shoes so much, we decide that to remain silent is to be kind.

The store attendants give us each a pin, for good luck. I'll manage to lose mine at the next stop, even though today is the day that I planned to leave my body behind. I want to stay in the present, focus on the details, I've said to myself. Forget any hurt. Forget the feet as they pound the gravel, the rocks, the pavement, the earth. Forget the back, the waist, the shoulders that carry the weight of the backpack. Forget the chin, with its black and purple marks, the small gash from that fall three days ago. But the body is still with me when I walk the path and my brain keeps wandering without following my eyes.

It's cold, cloudy, windy. *Will we get to Samos before the rain? When should we stop to eat? How far is the next town? I should look at my phone where I have a picture of today's route. I don't have enough energy today. How far is the next café?* And on and on my brain goes, making reach step more difficult.

Then something happens: I make an effort to look, instead

of just glancing ahead, at the trail. A ribbon of brown earth that extends forever, between tall trees, hunter green full canopies, next to a forest of thick green bushes, yellow and purple flowers, lichens and large black slugs under a darkening gray sky. I go inside. In order to stay in the present, I enter the past.

...

A Memory Shows Up – 1956

I was eight, my legs still dangled from the chair while I waited next to my mother for the dentist to be ready. Dr Ortelano, a gray-haired, kind woman, wearing a white apron. Maybe she was just forty years old, but to me she was old. I liked going to the dentist, then, fascinated by the foot driven drill.

There were no fast, electronic drills at that time, and there was even less use of anesthesia. Instead, Dr Ortelano pushed a pedal, which reminded me of my mother at her sewing machine, using a steady rhythm as she worked to repair a cavity. A simple, small, tooth decay required several sessions. Each time, we waited for a while in the sitting room. My mother read a magazine. I, bored to death, looked at the wallpaper, a pattern of forget-me-nots and stripes, and got lost inside the only picture hanging on the wall. A long gravel trail, a path between tall, dark green trees that seemed to extend to infinity. A perfect lesson in perspective.

Now I wonder, could I have had a cavity at eight? Maybe it was my mom's. Memory plays tricks after so many years. Still, I am sure about two things:

1. *I had a small crossbite, my top front teeth fitted on the inside instead of the outside of my lower ones. The dentist looked at them and said the bite would correct by itself. I just had to spend some time blowing balloons because that would help push out the top front teeth. Maybe she knew we didn't have money for orthodontia. (My top teeth still fall behind the lower ones, but nobody notices, except me. When I smile, you can only see my upper teeth)*

2. *I was at the same time fascinated and frightened by the infinite trail picture. The scene had an ominous air. I thought that at any time wolves might jump from the forest. I felt lost, but curious about what was at the end of that long path. There were no figures, no people in the picture, so I imagined a little girl, hidden between the trees. Could I make out her face in between the thick trunks? And was there someone coming down the path, so far away that I couldn't yet see, to harm her? Or to save her? I was sure that she had started to walk and couldn't find her way back...*

...

"Maria! Maria!" It takes a while to hear the voices. As if submerged at the bottom of a pool, my mind surfaces with effort back to the present reality. I turn to see that my friends stopped a while back. It's started to rain, and they are fretting about getting wet. I hadn't noticed. I guess I had managed to leave, even if only for a little while, my body behind. The rain jackets, the rain pants, the ponchos come out of the backpacks. There are self-congratulations all around about our preparedness. We've carried all this gear, all the weight on our backs, for eight days, just in case. Now we cover ourselves as if for a monsoon, although it turns out to be only a drizzle. The next town, Triacastela, is 30 minutes away, maybe less.

Inspiration

Inside my mother's bedroom,
I sit on the wooden floor
and listen to
the clicking noise,
the ritual afternoon sound
of the treadle sewing machine.
I whine, "I'm bored."
And then again:
"I've nothing to play with,"
I complain.
Her foot stops the back and forth
on the pedal.
She raises her green eyes,
from the small stitches,
joining blue fabric and white thread.

A pause, a moment,
and then, with pursed lips
and a frown,
"Use your imagination,"
she says,
and the stitching continues,
the fabric gliding
out of the machine again.

I'm eight years old,
a single child with freckles
and imaginary friends.

I stare at the specks of dust
that stream in the sunlight,
and scatter from my hands.

In the quiet afternoon,
my mother's foot
keeps on the pedal
that drives the wheel
that moves the fabric,
held tight by her hands
under the needle.

2nd Stage: Triacastela to Samos – Taxi Guilt

We walk, under the rain that is a drizzle. I'm pumped up, a story running inside my head, but it is already 5 p.m. and my friends lag behind. We are not used to wet weather, we have become California girls (that is what Daniel will call us when he sees us a few days later).

One of my friends makes a comment that starts as a whisper then, propagates. "We could take a taxi from Triacastela to Samos." "It is only a few more miles." "It wouldn't be cheating. There is no point in getting sick." "I want to see the Samos monastery, but we can do that tomorrow morning. Now is too late."

I know that I can keep going, but I can also enjoy a rest. "OK," I say. "Let's see if we can find a café in Triacastela and ask if they can get us a taxi."

After we walk another kilometer, we find a café. I talk to the lady behind the counter, who is nice and helpful. She orders a taxi for us. It will be there in 10 minutes. That is when Nelly says, "I'll go, but I don't want to take a taxi again." I believe it was she who didn't take well to the rain. It's an effort to keep my mouth shut, but I'm learning. I spend the wait watching four guys playing cards and laughing with each other. They play *truco*, a game I learned when I was a teen in Buenos Aires and have almost forgotten how to play. As I look at them, I try to inhale their joy, their calm, their *laissez faire*. I take pictures to remember. I think that what they do, or how they do it, must be a recipe for happiness.

The taxi driver is a woman, and I chat with her in Spanish.

She tells me about life in the town, the monastery, and in 10 minutes we are at the hotel. There is not much more than this modern hotel and the monastery in Samos. So, for once, after two difficult days, we relax for a moment, have a shower, dinner and sleep.

Playing truco *at Samos*

Flashback of regret, 1959

The day we arrived at the classy hotel in the mountains,
I had my blue polka dot swimsuit on before the bags were
    unpacked,
the dust from the long train trip was still in my hair and on
    my hands.
I had to wait for my mother to be ready — she was taking too
    long,
I thought, to get us settled.

I had a temper tantrum, I shouted, bawled, we struggled,
until I wore my father down, and he asked my mother to please
go with me to the pool.
He would take care of everything else.
The water was warm and transparent. I hugged my mother,
    coaxed her to smile.

Two nights later, during dinner, there was music.
My parents were good dancers,
but that night, they didn't dance.
The filet mignon, the champignons a la crème, the mixed salad,
remained untouched on my mother's plate.

I watched her protuberant belly,
No, she said, I'm not having a baby, you won't have a brother.
Please, take care of Dad when I'm gone.
I scratched the scar on my knee.
Why would she be gone?

*I was confused when we left the hotel
in such a hurry and went back home.
I was only ten.
The cancer was nimble and swift,
she died two months later.*

I never wore my blue polka dot swimsuit again.

Impatience

Samos to Sarria, Spain

May 8, 2019

A carved leg of a table inside the monastery

A Monastery in Samos

Today we will arrive at Sarria. Almost the midpoint of this journey. The walk from Samos to Sarria will make this a very long day. For my legs, but more so for my mind and my soul (does that exist?) During breakfast, Nelly repeats her comments about how many coffees I drink and about the need to have eggs in the morning. "If you really want them, they can probably cook them for you," I say. "No, this is enough. Not what I eat every day, but I like what I served myself." She continues, "I eat a banana every day for breakfast." There are no bananas today. Sometimes it is not what is said, but how it is said. I make an effort to keep my mouth shut, to be patient, gentle, leave my irritation aside, avoid rolling my eyes. I usually don't show my annoyance because I try to avoid controversy. I don't like altercations, disagreements, quarrels. I don't know how to deal with squabbles and I don't like to be disliked. We have a saying in the Argentinean vernacular, *porteño*, about people who complain, even if in a subtle way, about small things, about things that are not the way they think they should be. We call them *hinchapelotas*. The literal translation is *ball blowers*. People who are so annoying that they swell your balls (even if you are a woman and don't have those). I feel that this could be my friend Nelly today.

We start our walk going in the opposite direction to Santiago, our destination. The monastery looked majestic and enticing when we went past in a taxi yesterday. The taxi driver said that it was one of the oldest Galician monastic foundations dating back to the sixth century, that it had beautiful paintings inside. We want to visit it, but that means we have to back-track. After breakfast, just as we go out the door, Nelly says "We should have left earlier. It is 8:30 a.m., it might be too late." We go anyway.

The monastery has the largest cloister in Spain. Once we get there, we learn that for five dollars we can take a tour of the inside. Nelly says, "I won't take the tour, I'll wait on a bench outside." She seems in a foul mood. The rest of our quartet goes in. We learn that the monastery has nine monks and two novices now; it used to have many more. A fire destroyed a big part of it in 1951 and it was rebuilt in 1956-58 with the support of the community. I take pictures, want to remember the beauty of the place. The arches, the mosaics on the square that forms the cloister, the pictures on the walls, the furniture. The guide is nice and explains the history: some of the paintings are from after the fire, but others were preserved. There is an unusual table with its legs decorated at the top with the faces and wings of angels, and flowers, green and red, below. Even an antireligious person can find calm and pleasure in architecture, in silent cloisters surrounded by palms, green hedges enclosing small trees and clusters of yellow flowers. "Best use of five dollars," I say when we come out. I stop a few more minutes to check the chocolate made by the monks, but don't buy any.

The Last 100 Kilometers

The end result of the visit is that, as expected, we start our walk to Sarria in the late morning. There is an obnoxious attitude in the air, but I try my best. I go to the pharmacy with Nelly and help her get bandages for her blistered feet. I imagine that if my feet hurt, I wouldn't have a very good attitude either. Eventually, we make it to our first stop for lunch.

After we eat, Margaret and I, who walk at a leisurely pace together, get lost. In the end, we find our way and get to Sarria half an hour after our friends. This is an actual city, after so many small towns and unpaved roads and no cars. A city with hills and stairs. It takes us one hour after we enter its gates to find the hotel. On a corner, a yellow house, *La Posada de la Casona*, with a large lobby and a manager who is Uruguayan and has an Argentinean helper. Of course!

They recommend a place for dinner called Rome. Not the city, a restaurant. I guess the owner must be Italian, or they serve Italian food. Instead, it turns out that their specialty is *Chuleta de buey* — beef cutlet that is cooked on a large barbeque at the entrance to the restaurant. Almost a typical Argentinean dish, but I stopped the Argentinean meat diet after Enrique passed away. It was too difficult to cook or eat the beef, his preferred meal, with tears running down my cheeks.

Restaurant Dinner in Sarria

A gray evening. At the Rome restaurant
in Sarria, Spain, the waiter recommends
the ribs of pork or the lamb shanks.
But I no longer eat meat, I say.
Pimientos con queso then, over French fries?
Potatoes everywhere, potatoes again,
I don't eat those either. I don't want
to sound like a spoiled child. I can
eat anything else, I always find something I like.

"Maybe the *pimientos de padrón*, then?"
the waiter suggests: glistening green peppers,
drenched in olive oil, served with cheese,
calamari, lots of bread. Yes, I'll order that.
Even if I hate too much oil,
and I'm not sure about the cheese.
I can eat the calamari and the bread,
I think, but don't say.

The restaurant décor:
rough stone walls, like a cave.
While I wait to eat, and
while I eat, I observe.
At the entrance, a large grill,
the barbeque for the pork,
the shanks hanging in rows
from the ceiling.
And the lamb, or the famous *buey*.

And me, an almost vegetarian.
And yet, a feast for my eyes.
My heart is content. Not because
of the food, but the feeling
of home I get. It is the dark wood
of the walls. The grilled meat smells.

Afterwards, we slug our way back
to the hotel, me and
my three friends. We have walked
together many miles. Today,
a single block, under drizzle,
takes a long time.

Sarria

Sarria is the starting point for the people who do the "short" walk. We think that we are now seasoned hikers, having already walked about 100 kilometers; this last 100 kilometers should be a stroll in the park. There are groups of people milling around when we come down for breakfast, chatting about their concerns about the walk. They are just starting out. We give them advice and try not to feel smug, but we do. The guidebooks say, "Don't do it, don't feel superior because you have hiked more. Each person has their own Camino." A day later, we'll decide that we're not that seasoned after all, and that the easy going might be for those who do this stage in seven days. Our hotel plan calls for doing it in five.

Today We Should Rest

Sarria, Spain

May 9, 2019

Sarria

How We Rest

A rest day is for rest,
but not for me or my friends,
our enthusiasm is running high.
This city, Sarria,
is the midpoint
of our Camino
across Spain.
The city's few
sightseeing sites
keep our imaginations alive.
We, Margaret and I,
extricate ourselves
from the warm comfort
of the hotel.

Up and down the hilly streets,
over cobblestones,
under a gray sky,
drizzle and rain,
we walk 15,000 steps,
because this is our rest day.

It is just two of us —
our other two friends,
the N's
had an itch,
took a taxi to Lugo —
in the cold,

without warm jackets,
one wearing flip flops,
for the aching feet.
In the early afternoon,
they came back to the hotel,
to the warmth of their beds.

Margaret and I walk instead.
The whole day.
To the historical center.
To a little monastery,
Mostaire,
with a small cloister.
To several churches,
we see only from outside.
We say we would rather eat,
watch people,
chat, analyze,
than take a taxi or rest.

We end up
with a dinner of eggs
and beer, music
and smiles.
In the gray city,
under the gray skies.

Connection, Re-connections, Disconnections

Margaret and I walk up a hill, in the rain, ask a passerby about Calle Mayor, the historical district. I translate and then, as we follow the not-well-understood directions, Margaret and I just chat. We connect as friends, and with the world at large. We want to see the sights, to take pictures, to remember, to document what our minds will soon forget. At a restaurant by the river, where we stop for lunch — omelet and salad, with lots of bread, my usual fare these days — the server, who might be the restaurant manager or not, is a pleasant, middle-aged woman with short, light brown hair. In between taking orders and bringing plates, she sits at a table and feeds her grandchild — she tells us when we ask — a three-year-old boy with big amber eyes, and a head full of black curls. The child carries an iPad under his short arm and brings it to the table where he props it against a piece of wood. Afterwards, he focuses on the screen and works with it like a pro. His father, the server's son, with the same light brown hair and fair skin as his mother, stands behind the counter. He serves the drinks, works the espresso machine. We make up stories about the little boy's mom, a potential divorce, with no evidence except her absence from the café.

I listen to their language and think about prejudices, discrimination. We are in Galicia, land of Galicians, but we called them *Gallegos* when and where I was growing up. I find the sound of their Spanish musical, sweet with a hint of Portuguese. In South America, *Gallego* is a derogatory term, we made fun of their Spanish accent. Called them brutish, ignorant. This is how racism starts and ends.

Although I always thought of myself as open minded, someone who my conservative friends used to call "a bleeding-heart liberal," I have learned that there is, most of the time, an unconscious bias I drag around. A bias that I believe hides in most of us because it helps our brains make fast decisions. Often, we act based on that bias without giving our actions much thought. Travel sometimes helps to uncover our bigotry to ourselves.

I watch the white bartender father as he dances behind the counter. I watch the white grandmother feed her beautiful Black grandson. "Little one, a potato wants to enter your mouth and make its bed in your stomach," she says, and her Spanish sounds like music to my ears.

A Stereotype Destroyed by Accident – 1972

The summer after I got my PhD, I was twenty-four years old, and my husband and I took our first trip to Europe. Against my self-perception of being an unbiased, unprejudiced, liberal, multicultural person, I carried in my mind — unbeknownst to me — all the worst stereotypes from my childhood in Argentina. The Italians are loud (my father-in-law was Italian) and greasy (they oil their hair, a style at the time); the Germans are distant, authoritarian and most of them are Nazis; the French are dirty and drink too much wine; all Gypsies are thieves — I could go on. But I was lucky, I also carried with me all the books on the shelves of my father's bookcase and his love for people of any country, of any color, of any kind. Thus, that first time, after Enrique and I landed in Rome and drove to Venice, it wasn't the Italian stereotypes that I saw, but the magnificence of the plaza, the sound of the Italian songs. I sat at a café at the Plaza San Marcos in Venice and looked out over the large square, stunned by its beauty — all the pigeons around us, the basilica across in the foreground — and felt the tears form in my eyes and run unbidden down my face. That day, I, we, two poor graduate students, felt the wealth of the world in our empty pockets.

A year later, to celebrate my husband's PhD, we returned to Europe and drove from Italy through Austria, Hungary, Rumania, Yugoslavia (this was before the fall of the Berlin wall and Tito's death), France and Spain. One night, as we drove through Hungary on our way to Rumania, we collided with a horse-driven cart, swerved off the road, and came to a stop in a ditch. We were alone in the middle of empty countryside. However, soon many peasants appeared, it seemed from nowhere, and surrounded us. My first emotion was fear — I thought they would want to rob us. Instead, we soon understood, they only wanted to help us. The behavior of these farmworkers, of these simple country people, made me feel ashamed of myself.

As we traveled, our stereotypes were shattered, one by one — this is what travel does — and we were hooked on a never-ending journey. I still am.

I Wish to Be Her

The iPad has taken the place of the laptop on this trip where we have to travel light. I can't be — and I don't want to be — completely off the grid. There is this justification that I can edit the pictures, type what I write by hand in my journal every night. But even I know that is a lame excuse. I want to know my kids are OK, share my best pictures, and learn what is going on, at least every so often, with politics in the States, and yes, with my friends.

Once, when I went to Paris, I turned off all my media connections for two weeks. When I opened them again, I found death: two of my cousins had passed away. One of them I'd loved; with the other, I felt for his family, for what he had been. Of course, nothing would have changed if I had known earlier, but I felt as if it could have. That I could have helped. My head says: How could you, from miles away? But it felt wrong. So, no, I don't go off the grid for more than a couple of days at a time.

Today, a rest day, I have time and so I open the iPad to edit some of the recent pictures, upload them to media sites, telling myself that it's a way to keep my memories alive. I sit on the bed, in this large hotel room, with large windows facing the street corner. It's a blurred view, there's fog and rain outside. My mind wanders and I think I could write instead. I look for the last version of the chapter I wrote last month, but as I change windows, the photo application that I left open two weeks ago pops up. It has the pictures I took in Vietnam, six months ago, and that I had planned to edit, but never did. I scroll back, there are pictures of Morocco from eight years ago, when Enrique and I reserved there a room in a riad. The streets like labyrinths between concrete pink walls. The electrical wires like snakes slithering along the tops of the façades, no windows anywhere, just doors. No cars. I would take pictures of the doors whenever we went out so that we could find our way back.

I scroll some more, further back, and find Galapagos. There was that day we played with the sealions on the sand. Someone took a picture of both of us lying down, a sea lion by our feet. He had the wide brimmed leather Aussie hat, a red t-shirt and blue swim shorts. Nobody would have guessed he had been living with lung cancer for six years, but I knew. During that time, I was always on alert.

Now, I've forgotten where I am. I am inside the images, scrolling back and further back. Looking for me, and you, who we were. We are in Luxor, Egypt, where you were fascinated by how the columns in the temples still showed the colors from two thousand years ago. I was focused on the guys in worn linen *gallibayas*, posing next to us to be in the pictures and then ask for money afterwards. And here are those pictures from Sidney, Australia, at the opera, and with the kangaroos — that was when you bought that hat.

Further back — on Google all is possible. We are now in Hungary, in that crashed yellow Passat, and in Crete, on a motorcycle, until I'm looking at those pictures you took in 1969. All those thousands of slides you managed to convert to digital before there were film scanners or scanning services. Before you had trouble using your hands.

There I am, with long hair, no bags under my eyes, no wrinkles in my smile. The day we got married. I want to scroll back, I can't find the picture of that woman I was at fifteen, or twenty, when I was still growing up. I wish to be her one more time.

Then the iPhone pings. I get a text from Margaret. It is time to go outside, walk the streets of Sarria one more time.

Joy

Sarria to Portomarin, Spain

May 10, 2019

Green Fields

The Body Adapts

We start the day with obfuscation. The N's, Nelly and Nellie, have had an altercation. I can sense that something has happened between them, although no one is saying what it is. I always feel awkward and want to make everything nice when people are angry. It's as if they were angry with me, although I know otherwise. I want to ask what happened, but I'm wise and keep my mouth shut. It happened after breakfast, I think, which was scrumptious.

"Of course, the Argentinean culture," I said, when they served us dulce de leche and pancakes. Then came the cheese, cold cuts. It all looked delicious, but I only ate my yogurt with cereal and got some laughs. "You eat the healthy stuff, we eat the rest," they said. "I don't like to eat eggs or pancakes for breakfast," I said and then swallowed a spoonful of dulce de leche with gusto. "Cultural habits." I smiled.

The way is long, but it seems easier today. It's a bucolic landscape. A postcard of green fields with gentle hills, a stone church, a steeple in the distance, light brown cows along the way, a tractor tilling the land. I feel joy, a thumping of the heart, and my left brain asks the question: What is it in our cerebra that produces emotion, and why?

I grew up in a family that was secular but embedded in Jewish traditions. The symbol of the cross or a Christian church was viewed with indifference or disgust because, after all, Christians embody the persecution of our tribe. So then why the love, the contentment, the smile, the feeling inside my chest, the joy, when I see these churches? Any church, its steeples, the bird nests on its thatched roof, or the small shacks along the blooming fields, farmland. Is it just the simple architectural beauty? Plain nature? What is art?

In this stretch we encounter more walkers, hear more voices, different languages. All of them say, *"Buen Camino."* It translates as "good way," but it really means have a good journey. It is our hiking mantra. I find new friends, walk part of the way with a German girl on a break from school. She walks in sandals because, of course, hurting feet. A seasoned hiker, but not used to long stretches of pavement that we find every so often on this walk. I tell her that I am more used to asphalt and concrete than to gravel or soil. My practice is to walk the Strand, the paved strip next to the sand of the beach in the town I live. Then there is a guy from Finland, quite handsome. Rather than walk, he seems to run. And a couple from Spokane, newly arrived. We give advice.

At the end is the town of Porto Marin. But endings on this walk are never easy. To get to the hotel we must cross a very long bridge, with open railings that, together with the evening wind and my vertigo, test my resilience. I don't look down, just ahead, where many steep steps await to get to the hotel. If I do this, I can do that, I say. And I do. Joy returns. We all marvel at how the body changes in just eleven days. I eat more bread, I need the carbs, I have even started to eat more eggs, and the pads of my feet have grown thicker and harder, to cushion my body during the long walks. I no longer feel the weight of the backpack, and amazingly, I don't have the sciatic pain in my back.

Envy

Portomarin to
Palas de Rei, Spain

May 11, 2019

Guardian of the forest

Mantra

These last 100 kilometers are no easy stretch, not at 25 kilometers/day.

To avoid my morning annoyance, I hurry and try to go to breakfast earlier than everybody else. But I'm never the first. I have to live with comments like, "I want this to end," and, "I'll be happy when we make it to Santiago," when I want to say, "I enjoy the journey, every minute, I don't want this to end." But I don't say it. So, my lesson for today: *Just let go, get over it. Steady; if not the peace, keep the pace.*

Because it is a long walk, I chant a mantra to myself. *One step, two steps, one two three, uno, dos, tres.* Then I see three women ahead.

Envy Ahead

These three women,
they are all about my age,
they are overweight,
they don't even seem fit,
but they keep a good pace.
I watch them,
they are always ahead.
I have been chanting
uno, dos, tres, but
when I see them
I forget my mantra,
I want to catch up.
I hurry, I puff,
I swing my poles,
fast, faster I tell myself,
but they are still ahead.
They are not even fit,
they are overweight,
and they are still ahead.
Until I do it,
I manage to walk,
just next to them.
I look at them surprised.
They are all much
younger than I imagined
and they are nice and kind.
They all say, "Hello there,"
they wish me *"Buen Camino,"*

talk about the weather.
Why did I want to beat their pace?
And then, I'm ahead,
I no longer envy them.
I understand the game
my brain wants to play.
I just look for another signpost,
to help me keep the pace,
for the next 20 kilometers
ahead.

II: A Secret Date – The Lies We Tell

The longer Enrique and I went out together, the better we got along, the more we seemed to need each other, the further we were from being just temporary friends. Although that was the story I told myself. We liked to talk and to kiss, to be in each other's arms. One day we were thrown out of a café for making out in public. And yet, I felt that I had to keep lying, to keep hiding, so we enlisted the help of Jacobo.

Jacobo was a classmate of Enrique. He was Jewish, had a Jewish last name and, most important, he was a good friend. He would come and pick me up at home. When my father asked who I was going out with, or who was picking me up, I would tell him it was Jacobo. It was not a lie. After all, Jacobo was coming to pick me up, even if after a couple of blocks, he would leave me with Enrique and we would go, just the two of us, to the movies, to eat pizza, to sit in at a café and solve the problems of the world, several empty espresso cups and a full ashtray in front of us. I did feel guilty when I got back home, but I was happy, and I didn't know how to make it any better. If I told my father, he would ask about Enrique's family, notice that he wasn't "one of us," and I couldn't do that to my dad.

Two months after Enrique and I started going out together, my aunt invited me to go for the summer vacation to her apartment by the beach on the Uruguayan coast. I couldn't say no, and I don't think I wanted to say no, either. It was the type of vacation I always looked forward to, although maybe not so much that summer. But it was also a way to create some distance in a relationship I couldn't define to myself.

At that time there was no internet, a phone call between

countries was extremely expensive, and so we wrote letters. I asked Enrique to use his mother's last name in the return address; it was a last name of Dutch origin and sounded Jewish. I didn't want to invent a name, so this was consistent with my idea that I didn't lie. He laughed at my concern.

"Do you think she will care who sends you letters?" he said. "Are they so nosy?"

"They are Jewish, it is part of the culture," I said.

"I could write my first initial and they wouldn't know if I'm a boy or a girl."

"After the second letter, my aunt will ask why there is only an initial," I said.

Enrique's eyebrows curved upwards, he shook his head slightly, smiled and said — "OK, you know them better." He did as I asked.

As I expected, my aunt teased me as soon as the letters began to arrive for me every day. In the typical fashion of my family, she tried to find out more about the boy who was writing to me. Where did his family come from, what clubs did they go to, maybe she knew them? My aunt was kind and she tried to be unintrusive, but she was curious bordering on nosy. I told her, "He's just a friend." In truth, I think I was more worried about the effect that the family disapproval would have on my father than about how much my father would disapprove of my choice of boyfriend.

Half a year later, the students and teachers were violently removed from the academic facilities of the University by the Federal Argentine Police under orders of the federal government. Enrique and I were still going out together. Jacobo was still picking me up and my father thought that maybe Jacobo was my boyfriend, but didn't ask. That day, late in the evening, the police entered five University facilities armed with long batons and forced all the students and professors, some of them foreigners, who were still in the buildings to leave, all the while brutally beating them with the sticks.

The government wanted to purge the University of those who opposed the political intervention of the military government. It was particularly violent in the faculties of Exact and Natural Sciences and Philosophy and Literature. Many of my friends were there and were beaten and arrested. I didn't have classes that night and was safely at home. The event became known as "the night of the long batons," and after that, most of our professors resigned. I was at the end of my third year as an undergraduate in Physics, with still almost two years to go. The undergraduate degree in Physics took five years in Argentina. You finished with a Licenciatura in Physics.

We were left with a university with few professors, mainly those who agreed with the military intervention, most of them of mediocre quality. Enrique and most of his classmates, a year ahead of me, worried about how to keep progressing with their studies and what to do after they graduated; they started to write letters of application to universities in the U.S. and Europe. I had no idea what attending a university abroad meant, and I still had several classes to take before I could graduate, but I didn't want to be left behind. Enrique was fluent in English and one of the few among us who knew how to type. He wrote the letters for many of his classmates, and I said, "Me, too." The professors, out of work and going abroad themselves, wrote glowing letters of recommendation for all of us.

Should I say that I was unclear on the concept? That I didn't know that I was requesting to be accepted to a PhD program? That I was just being a follower, even if one who was quite good at physics and math? When I got accepted to several universities, I kept going through the motions, following the crowd, without realizing until almost the end what was going to happen. My father, who understood it better than I, was worried, but also happy because he thought it was an opportunity I wouldn't have had otherwise. He was the best father, so of course, although I tried to believe that I was just evading or deflecting the truth, I continued to lie.

I Entertain Myself

We walk and we march, and we hike, and we slug, and finally we stop. Just for water, bathroom, a snack. Most of the time there are stories playing inside my mind, while my eyes and my iPhone camera try to catch all the sights. Sometimes I chat with my companions, but I'm not that good at small talk, and we don't have the energy for deep conversations during these demanding hikes.

When we stop, it is at a place with a garden where we can sit on metal chairs under green canopies. I rest, silent, and watch the trail ahead, the grass all around us. While we sit, black and white cows go by, a few hikers following behind. I point the camera and take a short video to enjoy later, I tell myself. I want to stay and just absorb the peace, the sounds, but too soon, it's time to get up. We must forge forward, cross rivers over narrow bridges, follow the dirt path with no end in sight.

We walk between tall trees growing their new leaves. I'm ignorant of the tree names. I'll look them up, I promise myself, but I know that I will forget. I'm hungry, my feet hurt. I forgot to put them up at that last rest. I distract myself. There are so many people, now, on the trail. There is a guy walking in front of me who is dressed in a bright orange jumpsuit. I make up a story that someone told him that jumpsuits are what you must wear on the trail, that bright orange is good because it helps you to avoid getting lost. The whole idea makes me laugh and I take a picture. Again, to enjoy later, when I don't have to get anywhere, when I have more time. Although I know that I never have more time.

I observe the many hues, the colors on this path. The green of the baby trees, the yellow-green of parts of the grass, the green white of some leaves, the dark green-brown of the pines that stand further back, guardians of the forest where we won't dare to trespass. When Margaret walks a few steps away from the trail to relieve herself out of the public view, we keep watch. We don't trust the tree shadows, the lush canopies, we are city women.

There are yellow and purple flowers growing everywhere. There are white flowers blooming on the branches of the trees, and always, always, in this springtime landscape, the coffee brown of the tilled fields. And the greens of the lichens, the ferns, the ivy — who knows what else? I don't know their names.

After many turns, Margaret and I decide to have a last stop, get more water, rest a bit. We know that it always takes longer to get to the final destination than what is advertised in the guide. We sit and I drink an espresso, I don't like water that much. When we get up from the table, a guy at a faraway table makes signs at us, yells. I can't hear what he says. Margaret asks, "What did you forget?"

"Nothing," I say. We look around. He keeps making his signs and, at first, I wonder if he's either crazy or if he's flirting with us. I guess I'm still vain, I think that from 15 feet away I look younger than I am. Until it dawns on our slow American brains. We've set off on the wrong Camino, he wants to help us to avoid more pain. We thank him, profusely, from afar.

Orange jumpsuit on the trail

Casa Leopoldo

It's hot, and then not that hot. We walk, and walk, the walk that never ends, but eventually we do get to our destination for the day. It's Casa Leopoldo, a quaint pension on a side street. We, the M's, get there a few minutes after the N's. The manager, a youngish woman wearing an apron, her hair tied back, and with a somewhat harried look, would like to register the four of us together, get our names, give us the keys and then take us to our rooms, all on the first floor. But Nelly can't wait, she insists on going to her room right now, her feet can't take it anymore. Margaret and I look at each other; we feel a bit embarrassed. I apologize to the pension host. "Our friend is suffering from a bad case of blisters on her toes," I say in Spanish. The poor woman gives up, climbs up with the N's and their duffel bags, and then she comes down to complete the registration for Margaret and I. She is nice and very kind.

"You have dinner in a great restaurant that is just three blocks away. It is really close," she says. I believe that the town is so small that it is probably the only restaurant.

My room is tiny but cozy, with a window to the street and a row of bright pictures on the cream-colored wall. It has a narrow and short twin bed against the wall, a little table in a corner and a closet-sized bathroom into which the shower, the toilet and the sink barely fit. I set my carry-on under the table and when it is open, I have to hop over it to reach the bathroom.

Part of me enjoys the tight embrace of the small room, it reduces the choices. I feel a peace of mind. Part of me loathes the lack of comfort. And this ambiguity gives me anxiety. I know that it is only for a night, but I'm a princess at heart. I'm also a bleeding heart who knows how much I have and that I wouldn't like to give it up.

We have time to shower and rest before we go for an early dinner. We are so tired we think we might fall asleep eating. But we are rewarded with an amazing meal of octopus with lots of bread, and sangria that lights up my friends' smiles. I can't see my own.

After dinner, the server brings a slice of cake and pours a liquor on top. Margaret opens her eyes wide, I take her picture and we all laugh. It gives us enough energy that before we go to bed, we decide to go by a store that sells knick-knacks to buy gifts and un-needed stuff. Then we remember our bodies and go by the pharmacy and buy moleskin and tape for the feet, and I get eye drops for my dry eyes.

Casa Leopoldo room

Pillow Lace

In this quaint hotel, the fabric covering the pillow is soft, and when I go to sleep, I rub my fingers against each other through the uneven material to feel the texture. It is a sensual pastime, a kind of masturbation I have had with some fabrics since I was very young. Sometimes it brings me peace, sometimes it brings me memories.

When my mother got sick, my rich uncle, her older brother, brought her a silk robe from Europe. It was a hope against hope that it would bring a smile to her pale face, a healing to a terminal disease. The robe was green, turquoise like her eyes, with a cream and raspberry pattern; it reached her ankles. It had a couple of shimmering nacre buttons on the front placket, a wide sash at the waist. A textured material that looked and was expensive, she could have worn it to a party, if she had had the strength. Instead, it was her dress up robe during her last two months of life, while she went in and out of the hospital, in and out of bed to the bathroom and back. It was imbued with her essence, and her perfume.

When my mother died, I didn't cry. I didn't know how. Instead, I just held my father's hand and stared at her immobile shape on the hospital bed. Her skin was clammy to the touch and she had cotton in her nostrils. "They should have taken those out," was the only thing my father could say.

Four years later, I sat cross-legged on the floor inside my parents' closet. The robe was still hanging there. I was in their bedroom, my father's bedroom now, my mind riding the soundless shadow of time. Listening to the inner voice of intense guilt that would not go away.

The day I locked myself in the bathroom. My mother shaking the handle.

"Let me in."

"No."

"Why did you do it? You have bad manners," she said

The fight was already over, and I no longer remember what it was about, just that I was angry, mad at her.

"Let me in, I'm telling you for the last time."

"I wish you were dead," I said. That was it. And I couldn't take it back. I had let the evil out into the world.

Silence.

"I will not spank you, let me in."

I opened the door, hugged her. Cried. But I knew that my thoughts were powerful. I was only ten. My mother died four months later. I couldn't put the genie back in its bottle.

My index and middle finger play with the fabric of the silk robe. I soothe myself with its touch. I put my head inside its folds and smell her perfume, still there after all this time. I want to bring her back, but she is no longer there. The silk robe hangs next to her old brown felt housecoat. Why are her clothes still hanging in my father's closet? For many years, he didn't touch anything of hers. He couldn't. He didn't talk about her either.

The usual routines, the everyday things, do not stand out as much as the few unusual occasions. I touch the brown felt, it feels like the old apartment. It feels like my shouts when I was mad. The kitchen smelly because the sewer backed up most of the time. The toast with butter and marmalade for breakfast. The days I spent reading or talking in my head. When I slept in the living room on a daybed and fell asleep chatting with invented friends while my parents chatted between themselves in a language I couldn't understand.

The robe, the housecoat, forty years later, those clothes are still hanging inside my mind while I rub my index and middle finger against the lace of the pillow slip in this quaint hotel, lulling myself to sleep in the middle of a Spanish night.

Endurance

Palas de Rei to Melide
to Arzua, Spain

May 12, 2019

A nap in the middle of the hike

Mother's Day

My word for today was endurance. It was 30 kilometers up and down. A walk that left the bottoms of my feet hurting more than the previous 10 days had. I started the day thinking, "Endurance with joy," but I went through stages of pity, envy, jealousy, contentment, joy, pain, gluttony, greed, anxiety, excitement, and ended with gratitude. Gratitude to be alive, to be able to walk so much, but also to have found a way to do this with three other women who are different from me in many ways, and not different in so many others.

As we go up the uphill path, we meet two young Taiwanese girls, May and Maple. I think at first that they're twenty years old, but it turns out that they are thirty-something. One has a five-year-old child. They are hip, laugh and jump instead of walking, and take selfies with us. We watch them and I wish we could be that age again. Then I think, not just that age, but also so free to be who they are. It took me years to understand who I was, and I am still working on it.

When we meet again on our next rest at a café, one of them asks about my pants. "I love them, where did you buy them?" May asks. We laugh. I first say, "Oh, they are very expensive, one of a kind." They look at me and want to know where, how much. I can't maintain the lie. Margaret is laughing so much.

"I bought them at Target," I say.

"Target?" they repeat. "Really? They are so chic."

Afterwards they want to know my age. "I'm older than you," I say with a smile. They are too young; I can't tell them my age. We tell them the story of how, when a seasoned hiker recommended these pants, and Margaret found them in Target and sent me a picture, I said they were the ugliest pants I had ever seen, and although they were cheap enough to buy them, just in case, I swore I would never wear them. Now, I'm planning to put them on every day.

My kids have just sent texts for Mother's Day. Avatar bitmojis, with hearts and laughs. They are big on bitmojis. They are men, do not like to show too much emotion. Bitmojis are as far as they go. I think that for them, logical and analytical boys, I'm their mother, so why have a special day? If you love your mother, it doesn't matter the day. After all, it's a commercial invention to sell flowers and cards, improve the economy. And of course, if you don't like your mother, why be hypocritical and show love during a single advertised day? I don't question the love of my children, but these days I need as much affection as I can get.

Later, I meet an Italian man from Lucca who is walking with his seven-year-old son. I practice my poor Italian and tell him, "What courage you have! To do this with a child!" I take a picture of the two of them, walking as fast as we are, talking all the way. The mother couldn't make it, he tells me, she had to stay at home for work. I want to keep talking, I'm nosy and curious about the lives of strangers. But they stop for a moment, and I continue, too shy to stay inside their private conversation.

We walk further and I see a guy taking a nap with his dog on the grass at the side of the path. He opens his eyes and smiles when we pass. He looks content and relaxed. I take a picture, I want to document his bliss. "Don't you wish we had enough time to take a nap on the grass?" I say to Margaret, who is walking by my side. But we have to hurry up, get to our next hotel before dark.

Feet

Arzua to Rua O'Pino, Spain

May 13, 2019

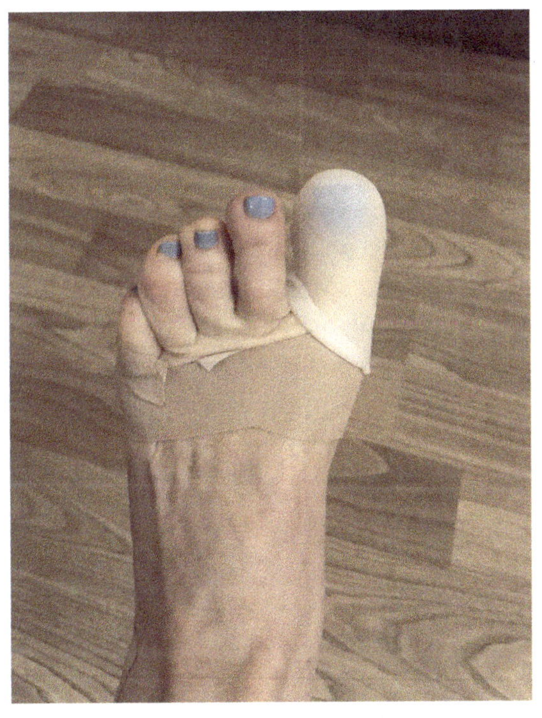

Iron Feet protected by tape and a toe condom

Iron Feet

It is the evening before the last day. We are resting with a group of other hikers on the patio of our hotel in Arzua. About four or five women and one man, we lounge on comfy couches covered in rough, white and blue striped fabric. Our naked feet rest on a glass coffee table at the center of our circle. We have finished dinner, and for once it is still early and we are so close to the end that we are able to relax and chat.

But I can feel the emotion, the trepidation, the elation going around. The excitement is in the words we say, the laughter we share, the air we exhale. We compare feet, blisters and pedicures, then share tales of grief, pain, courage and joy.

Our fellow travelers come from all over the world and we call them by their places of origin, even when we learn their names. Sturdy and fast, "Montreal" has a weak knee. "I could barely finish the last kilometer," she says as she pulls up her hiking pants and shows her black knee brace. We're surprised to see her as vulnerable and sweet. We'd thought her haughty and aloof, just because she wouldn't smile that much, or she rushed to arrive first.

The two "Wales" friends, Marge and Angela, sit together with blissful smiles on their faces. Angela has a soft cast on her ankle. Marge watches us watch Angela's leg. "Angela broke her ankle in February," she says. "It was a freak hiking accident. But we didn't want to cancel the trip, we decided to go ahead with this journey anyway."

I watch the two friends, one dark haired, the other showing some white. They must be in their fifties. "How can you hike if your ankle is not healed yet?" I ask. Marge and Angela take turns telling their story.

"We had been planning it for such a long time," Angela says.

"She didn't let me cancel. Angela limps by bus from hotel to hotel and cheers me up when I leave in the morning and welcomes me with a drink when I arrive later in the evening," Marge says.

We learn later that Marge lost her husband last year. I wish I had a friend like that. Then I think: Maybe I do; after all, I have three friends who have walked with me all this time.

"Harrogate" (he's our friend Daniel from England, whom we found almost a week ago) lost his wife last year. In blue ink and a stunning cursive, he writes in a journal every day; he carries a portable printer in his bag and every evening prints the pictures he took during the day. Then, he glues them into the journal — his way of honoring the memory of his wife, who used to trek all over the world with him.

"Finland" hiked part of the way on bare feet because he had a painful rash on his toes. He's the handsome guy who does yoga after he stops to rub cream on his toes. Which gives us a chance to stare at his athletic body and take pictures on the sly. Later, we see him running, black leather shoes back on. "How are your feet?" I ask. He gives me the thumbs up, too focused on the next goal post to stop to chat.

The feet that we rest on the coffee table, they are a key body part during this crazy hike. The feet don't do so well for the three friends who came with me from California. Two of them have unpleasant blisters, white things near their nails. The third has a weak arch she tapes every day. I'm amazed how they keep going; strong and stubborn women, they will get to the end. When we get back, I'll learn that all of them have lost a few toenails.

Me? I have a scarred heart and iron feet. I rub writing on my heart; the memories I jot down every day seem to lessen the scar. The feet? They are fine. Wide, well padded, with fat toes that look like sausages, German sausages. They aren't pretty, but they are functional. When I was younger, I wished for the narrow, dainty feet of my friends who could wear the popular ballet flats. When I tried the trendy stiletto sandals in my twenties, my poor toes felt and looked like encased sardines, so I gave up and was happy when Doc Martens became the thing. Still, I always wanted to have slim feet. Today, in my boots, these feet are my best asset. They have carried me over two hundred kilometers with no blisters or noticeable damage. Iron feet.

Crime and Punishment – 1958

During the second week of December 1958, last days of spring in the southern hemisphere, when the school year was about to end, my parents and I moved from our cramped one-bedroom apartment in a lower middle-class part of town to a modern, larger, two bedroom, two bath, plus maid quarters apartment, in upper middle-class downtown Buenos Aires.

We needed new furniture. My father ordered a custom bookcase for the living room. The bookcase was made of polished clear oak wood, carved decorative curlicues on its sides, inlaid moldings on its top and bottom. On one of the upper shelves, he set his hardbound books. Their leather covers had golden letters on their spines. I loved to look at them from across the room, intrigued about their contents. The shelf was higher than I could reach on my pointed toes. I think the idea was to keep them out of reach of children. They were adult books.

The cabinet had a set of doors near the base that hid a new record player and my parent's collection of vinyl records. "You have to clean your hands before you touch the records," my father said. Followed by, "Do not use the record player. The needle or the record can be scratched if you are not careful!" It was a forbidden action I didn't question.

After much discussion, my parents also got a sectional couch that would fit in a corner across from the bookcase, and an armchair. The sofa was upholstered in a blue boucle fabric; it had tiny loops, circlets that were rough to the touch, but pleasant to look at. With firm cushions, you had to sit with your back straight. The armchair, on the other hand, was brown leather, smooth and comfy. The leather was cold in winter.

During summer, a humid, scorching season, the leather would stick to the damp bare skin of my legs in shorts.

Then there were the long conversations about the pillows for the hardwood benches in the kitchen breakfast nook. What color, what fabric, what texture. My mother would make them; she was good with patterns and the sewing machine, and she sewed all my dresses. Since we would be going soon on our summer vacation, she planned to buy the fabric and make the pillows when we returned, while I was at school.

In January, we left by train for the mountains, in the province of Cordoba. A green place, with clean air, a hotel with a swimming pool. We were excited, I was full of expectations. We planned to get back in February, get ready for the school year. At the beginning of March, I would start fifth grade at a new school, in the new neighborhood.

But in the middle of April, I still hadn't started school. My home, my father, my world was in chaos. A few classmates from my old school, the one I had attended until the end of 4th grade, came to visit. I thought they came just because they were my friends, but it was a visit of sympathy. I had lost my mother two weeks before. They sat on the sofa, tried the armchair, looked at the books, and stared at a picture on one of the shelves. It was a picture in colors, at a time when most pictures were black and white. The picture of my father, my mother and me against the green backdrop of the hotel where we had gone for our vacation. "Do you have a brother?" my classmates asked. I didn't. They all had siblings, and two parents. After they left, they never came back again.

One week later I started school, a late start when all the girls had already formed their friendships. My father worked; I didn't make new friends easily. In the afternoons, I would come home to lunch, a maid, and silence. I felt alone in the house. So, one afternoon, I climbed on one of the dining room chairs and pulled down a heavy hardcover book, one with a beautiful blue leather cover, thick with many very thin, silky pages that gave me pleasure to turn. The sounds of the street came through the open window, the breeze stirred the curtains, but the house was still. I opened the bookcase doors and searched the records until I found one with a bright yellow cover. Careful to settle the needle on one of its grooves, I turned the record player on. Then I sat in the armchair and read. The book was Crime and Punishment. The record, Vivaldi, the Four Seasons. I heard the same record over and over again every afternoon until I got to the last thin page of the book and the school year came to an end. I was only ten years old. Many decades later, the music and book are still engraved in my mind. Do I think I am a superwoman; do I want to punish myself for the guilt I feel about my mother's death?

My mother no longer there, my father never noticed or cared that I touched his books or his records. We never had pillows for the hard wood benches as we sat in silence for each breakfast, lunch and dinner at the kitchen table.

Grief

Last night,
grief raised its ugly head.
He wants to be my partner
during the rest of this journey,
now that I'm near the end.

Sorrow and sadness
interrupt the wonder.
All the green hues,
so vivid yesterday,
grow dark.

I walk in the shade,
under a sunny sky.
The tulip poplars,
their branches covered
by green foliage
and cup shaped blooms.

I look for my partner,
the one who held my hand,
my friend from so many journeys.

Instead,
the path is empty.
I feel the angst
of the end of the road.
A hollow feat,
no one to share it with.

I have been here before.
Change the rhythm,
secure your stride,
try a sprint,
or stop and observe.
Endure, I tell myself, again.

Then I pass the white sheep
and hear their bleating.
The heart does a skip,
I step, step, step,
one more time.

This is not the end.
The end only comes
when there is no more life.
And I'm still alive.

This time my step
is a dance
of thanks,
I'm amazed to be
one more day
on this earth,
standing up.

PART III

The End – Ashes to the Sea

We're Here

Rua O'Pino to Santiago, Spain!!

May 14, 2019

O'Pino to Santiago trail

How We Reach Santiago

It is the last day, or one of what will be many "last days." We will reach Santiago today. We walk and walk and then stop to have lunch, which is when the heat starts to press down on us, the trees become scarce, and the trail becomes concrete underfoot. We sit and eat omelets and salads in the shade. I have been eating more omelets than I care to count during this trip, but they have been the best I have ever had. The fresh eggs have a yellow-orange color and a scrumptious taste. "I will miss these eggs," I say. I think that what I really mean is that I will miss this walking pace, this communality with nature that is missing from my daily California life.

We start again at 2 p.m.; the heat is worse. Margaret has blisters on her feet and needs to go slowly. The N's have disappeared in their anxiety to get there-there, to the hotel in Santiago, to get their feet up. I'm amazed at Nelly's endurance, at how she can command her hurting feet to carry her without stopping to get sooner to the end. I have a different spirit inside me; I can be stoic, but I have to give some space to my pains, or maybe it's space to allow the daydreams of my brain.

We walk at a steady pace, but what we thought would be an easy trail becomes an ascent — to Mount Gozo, the Hill of Joy, another nine, 10, 12 kilometers. But who's counting? This is supposed to be our last hill and last stop before we reach the Cathedral of Santiago de Compostela — where we should cry in rapture at finally seeing the end of our path. I think that I will just raise my trekking poles, take a few pictures and a deep breath. Maybe allow myself a sigh of gratitude to have gotten that far.

When we reach Mount Gozo we stop and make a victory sign.

"Easy peasey from here on," I tell Margaret.

"All downhill from now on," she replies. I'm running on the pure trill of anticipation, of getting there soon.

But it will be another hour at a regular pace from Mount Gozo to Santiago. It is very hot, Margaret and I walk and stop to drink water, and walk and stop again to go to the bathroom. We now walk on concrete. We finally make it to a plaza with a big sign that says Santiago de Compostela. We think that the hotel is around the corner and take pictures of the sign, and of each other, but this is just the gate to the city. We are on the outskirts of the city, and we don't know it yet, but it will be another long hour before we get within sight of the cathedral.

Missing But Not Lost

We walk through the plaza with the big Santiago de Compostela sign and keep our steady but slow pace under the heat, on the pavement, crossing streets with lots of cars and buses, stores and people. I find this strange, after the quiet of the fields, and the small villages. I'm not surprised at my annoyance with the busy city. It's part of my ambiguous make up, and this trip has helped me to learn more about myself. I'm a city girl, a city woman who loves city life, but who also needs the silence, the trees and large stretches of green, to find herself and to feel content. After we have walked almost an hour, the landscape changes, the city becomes a small town, and when I look up, I see in the distance a top shaped like a bell with Baroque spires. It sits at the top of winding streets, a hill we still have to climb. This is my first view of the Santiago de Compostela cathedral. My breath stops for a moment. I feel awe, I'm exuberant. I even take a few dancing steps in the middle of the street.

"We made it!" I hear myself yell and I turn around to give a victory sign to Margaret. Also, to show whoever may be looking at me, although nobody is, that I'm not crazy. That I'm just a bit happy-drunk and I'm traveling with a friend who feels the same.

But Margaret is not anywhere behind me. I've lost Margaret! Has she been kidnapped; did she fall, and I didn't hear? I scream her name in the middle of the street, retrace my steps with panic on my face. Now people do look at me, probably thinking I'm deranged. I feel I'm acting a bit paranoid but I am also scared. I try to calm my fear, a well-known fear of loss that rises from my gut to my brain and back. I ask a woman nearby, who is walking with a girl, "Did you see a hiker with a hat, a woman, tall. A royal blue backpack?" She moves her head no. I notice that she tries to not make eye contact with me. I don't want to scare her, but I'm scared myself. Then I ask a guy standing in front of a store. Nobody has seen her.

I use my cell to try to call her, but her phone, I know, is in her backpack and she might not hear it. I text the N's: "I have lost Margaret." They think I'm joking. "We are here at the hotel, in the jacuzzi," Nellie texts back. "It's the best. Are you almost here?" Nelly adds with an emoji smile. I don't know how to make them understand my distress, and then I think, what purpose would it serve if I could?

However, after a few minutes Margaret hears her cell inside the backpack and answers my call. "All of a sudden I didn't see you ahead, and I figured that I just took a wrong turn," she says.

"I'm on the street that goes directly to the Cathedral. I can see the spires from here," I tell her. "I'm standing in front of a yellow cylindrical mailbox. It says *Correos* on the side in big letters."

"I'm around the corner," Margaret says with a chuckle.

I breathe, feel relieved. When we meet again, I laugh and tell her: "I wondered how anybody could get lost when the cathedral cupola can be seen at the top of the hill?" And so, tired but amused and content, we continue toward the center of Santiago and our final destination, the Parador hotel.

Although we now can see the cupola of the Cathedral all the time, pointing our way ahead, it takes us almost another hour before we get to its front steps and to our hotel. Our walk is still slow in the heat and over concrete, but we no longer complain. Of course, just at the end, I, the smart navigator, decide that the arch we can see at less than 50 m distance, with lots of people milling about, is just a tourist sight, not really the entrance to the Obradoiro Square where we have to go.

"Let's take this shortcut," I say. The "shortcut" turns out to be a "longcut" that takes ten extra minutes, as we walk around the outside of the old medieval wall surrounding the city of Santiago de Compostela. We could have walked directly under the arch instead.

"I chose the scenic route," I joke, when we finally come out of an alley, turn right and find the Square, the Cathedral on one side, and at right angles the façade of the Parador hotel.

When we walk up to the Parador entrance, through an intricately carved doorway, above which are the busts of the Catholic monarchs, Ferdinand II and Isabela I, our faces can no longer contain our smiles. It must be contagious. As we register at the front desk, even the receptionist beams a wide grin at us, and we all start to laugh. Then, we look around almost in reverence at the lobby, the tapestries, the antique furniture and the seventeenth and eighteen century artworks, the stone archways leading to several cloisters and, further down, to our rooms. There is magic in this place, history on its walls, a marvel, our treat after the long hike.

Margaret and I high-five each other. No, I don't cry, but I think that my laugh has tears of joy inside it. We can't believe that we will be staying at this place for three nights.

Parador de Santiago arrival

A Magical Place

As tired as I am, dragging my bags across one of the hotel's cloisters to my room, I stop to take pictures and wander around, checking the stone walls, the glass covered printed papers describing some of the history of the place. This cloister is a large square with arches, covered with engravings, on each side of the patio, and a stone fountain with tritons sitting in its middle. I learn that this is one of four cloisters that comprise the hotel.

The room, once I get there, is enormous, with carved wooden furniture, a very large king bed, a jacuzzi bathtub and a shower. I undress and take a long bath while I exchange texts. My three other companions are doing the same. We plan a post-rest celebration dinner in one of the magnificent restaurants of the Parador de Santiago.

While I dress and put my bag away, I read the parador guide. It says that, according to the Catholic tradition, if you faithfully complete the arduous trek to the Finisterre (the end of the earth), your sins will be forgiven. I also read that in the Middle Ages, wealthy aristocrats would often hire people to walk in their name in order to be absolved of their sins without setting foot on the Camino. I think that I have walked with my memories all the way; should they be absolved as well?

Later that night we have our celebration dinner with Daniel, the friend we met a week ago, ages ago, in Villafranca, at *la Puerta del Perdón*. We sit at the table and as we cheer and congratulate each other before our first sip of wine, I say, "We are all perdonados (forgiven, without sin) now, even if we have not yet reached the end of the earth."

Everybody laughs. I don't know if it's because they like my joke or if it's a nervous laughter. Maybe Daniel or my other friends have walked because they feel guilty about a particular sin. I know that there is a part of me, hidden under layers of clowning and witticisms, that doesn't want to emerge. Maybe it's the spiritual part of my being fighting to be heard.

We eat at one of the two restaurants of the Parador de Santiago. It's a restaurant so grand, so filled with history and tradition, luxury and beauty, that it makes me feel as if I'm alive in the Victorian era and very rich. I eat all the bread. And then, when we go out and hear the music, I dance in the Plaza. I do not have an epiphany or a revelation, but I feel joy. I dance and dance. I tell myself, "That is my spirit."

The next day, while we're relaxing and touring a bit of the city, Nelly says she doesn't like the hotel. "It's like Disneyland," she says. It's not, I think, but I don't say so. Once again, I don't want to enter into an unnecessary argument. To each their own beliefs.

And yet, I can't resist, I do explain: "This is an historical building that used to be a hospital. Its construction was started in 1499. There is nothing fake here, except the upgrades to make it a hotel. The whole city is history come alive." I'm angry, I feel like I have to protect the building and its history. There must be something embedded in my psyche that makes me revere art and tradition and feel awe at the sight of Gothic influenced architecture. I dig inside, but can't find where it comes from, except from an odd respect for culture and age.

Afterwards, Nelly is embarrassed to be in the selfie we want to take of all of us on the little tram that tours the city. "I don't want anybody to know we did the tram tour," she says. "I hate to be an American tourist." We are tourists, I think, when I look at her carrying a lemon-yellow hiking backpack, dressed in a long skirt and flip flops, carrying a yellow-orange leather bag and drinking from a bladder, but of course, I don't say it. Each one of us has her own demons to deal with and who am I to judge? Myself? I like to be a child, laughing, touring through old cobble stone streets inside an electrical train.

III: A Secret Undone – I Confront My Lies

It must have been around April 1967 when I received a thick envelope in the mail. It had been stamped Cambridge, Mass. It came from the U.S. and for a moment I speculated about who could be writing to me, I didn't know anybody there. Once I opened it and read the cover letter, it took me a while to understand what it said. My English wasn't very good. But when I managed to decipher the sentences, I was astonished. I hadn't anticipated that we would get a reply to our applications to the American universities. I almost took it as a game, wishful thinking. Most of the application work had been done by my boyfriend, Enrique, who knew English and how to type. I had just given him my information and the transcripts and signed the request. I re-read the letter and, although I was aware that my heart was beating fast, I wasn't sure how I felt. Excited? Curious? It said that MIT, the Massachusetts Institute of Technology, was offering me a place for the fall. I didn't know where Massachusetts was, let alone what the offer meant.

"I got a letter from MIT," I told Enrique. I called him as soon as I figured out most of the words in the letter. "They are offering me a place to study there."

"I got one, too," he said. "And another from Kansas State. There should be more coming soon." He sounded euphoric. "Check your mail tomorrow and let me know. We have our pick."

I was hesitant, diffident, uncertain. And yet, some part of my brain was telling me that this was something good. I had to re-read that letter to find out what I had to do to follow up.

I thought about how I would tell my father that I would be going away, far away. I didn't know how he would respond when I told him. I was anxious that he would be desolate, he would think I was abandoning him, leaving him alone. I didn't realize that he had been following my comings and goings and he was prepared, he knew my decision before I made it myself, he was ready to support me in anything that could improve my brain and my future, even if it was agonizingly difficult for him. He was a good father. I was a bad liar.

Once we got the letters from the other universities — there were four or five in all — I not only had to make the decision of whether to attend one of them, but if I did, which one. Enrique wanted to go to a good university that offered an assistantship. I was interested in the location. I wanted to be near the ocean. We discussed options.

"I like MIT, but it only offers an assistantship after the first semester and only if we do well. We would have to have our own support for six months." Enrique said. "I don't have that kind of money."

"I don't know if I can do well enough the first six months," I said.

Two days later we studied a map together. A large paper map from the National Geographic that had been folded and refolded many times and had very small print. Enrique's father had subscribed to the National Geographic for many years. Unusual at that time in Argentina, but he liked to travel. Both of Enrique's parents were traveling in Europe when we extended the map over the living room table in Enrique's house. A round table made of superb mahogany wood that was always covered with a linen tablecloth so it wouldn't get damaged.

"Look," I said, "the University of Maryland, in College Park, is almost next to the Atlantic." I guess I didn't quite get it that, while it looked close on the map, the ocean was about four hours away by car. Enrique knew how far it was, he read maps better than I did, but he didn't say. He liked the U. of Md. for a different reason. It had a good standing as a school of physics and astronomy and offered both of us free tuition and the best assistantship of all the offers from the other universities we applied to, starting as soon as we got enrolled. We agreed, we should go there. Still, it would take a while until we could get everything in order. I had to finish my last year of undergraduate in December. We had to each get a student visa. Enrique had to take a final test.

It took me some effort to tell my father. "It will be for just one year," I said. We both believed that was the truth. He was only worried about my safety, and I told him I would be going with two friends. They would be my chaperones. One of them was Enrique, the other had a Jewish sounding last name. I didn't disclose that I had been dating one of them, the one with the non-Jewish name. However, I think my father had started to suspect. Perhaps he thought, as I did myself, that it was a temporary relationship — although when I arrived in the States, in January of 1968, it had been more than two years since Enrique and I had started to date.

For another year, while attending graduate school at the University of Maryland, we kept going together, sleeping together, but living apart for appearances' (parents') sake. After all, it was 1968. I had found a couple of American roommates who managed to earn the trust of my father, he thought I would be safe staying with them. I think they were learned in the art of deception.

The day I took my father to visit the apartment and the potential roommates, every room was tidy, the kitchen and the bathroom were gleaming, squeaky-clean. The kitchen-sink still had soap bubbles swimming around the garbage disposal flange, and everything smelled fresh. There was a vase with yellow mums on the table. Only one roommate was at the apartment, and she was dressed like a perfect schoolgirl, with a pleated *skirt and a white long-sleeved blouse. She wore no makeup and opened the door to the apartment with a welcoming smile.*

"My father is not quite sure about this arrangement. He worries because I will be by myself so far away," I told her after we had exchanged some pleasantries.

She looked first at me and then at my father and said, in English with bits of Spanish so he was able to understand:

"My family lives one hour away. They always check on me and they will help us if we need anything."

My father loved her at first sight. Of course, as soon as I started living there, the cleanliness decreased a bit and the clothes changed to cut-off jeans and t-shirts. My roommate's family never showed up. My father never learned that the second roommate had a drug addiction, but fortunately she was almost never at the apartment and decided to leave before the first semester ended.

Soon after I started my classes, I realized that the program I was in wouldn't end in one year. That it would be at least four or five years before I graduated. About some things, I wasn't smart, or maybe I was good at lying to myself. After a while, I had to tell my father that I would not be able to use the return ticket that was valid for only one year. He was a pragmatic man; he managed to exchange it and use it to visit me later in the U.S. instead.

Before the end of the winter semester of my second year, the only remaining roommate had decided to get married. I would have to look for a new roommate; I felt I couldn't lie to myself anymore. Enrique and I began to discuss that maybe instead of me getting a new roommate, we could get married. I no longer remember well the timeline of events, but I know that just at that time my father came to visit.

I was glad to see him after such a long time. I wanted to show him all the good parts of my life in the U.S., including my friends. I planned trips to nice tourist spots and both Enrique and my other Argentinean friends came with us. My father liked to be among my friends, and he and Enrique got along well, they shared jokes and smokes. They say that you tend to marry your father, if you are a girl, or your mother, if you are a boy. And although at that time I thought that Enrique couldn't be more different from my father, looking back I realize how similar they were in so many ways. Both of them secular, curious, extremely honest, able to see the ironical side of life and unable to stand B.S. Both of them were also life-long smokers.

One day when my father and I were sitting in a coffee shop near the University, I blurted out before I could repress myself, "I like Enrique, we are dating, and we want to become a couple, maybe get married." We had just finished a lunch of hamburgers and French fries and I still had the smell of charbroiled meat mixed with grease in my nostrils. I didn't like hamburgers too much, but for my father it was a novelty.

We were sitting across from each other on orange plastic chairs, and we had in front of us, sitting on top of the white Formica table, big mugs of coffee. I stared at a brown stain on the tabletop; I could almost make the shape of a heart. My father took a sip from his cup. In his face I saw an expression of distaste. "I can't stand the weak coffee they serve here," he said, but his eyes showed sadness more than disgust. He said, "I don't have anything in common with his family, they are not mishpucha." [6] *However, he didn't say, "Don't do it," or, "I don't like him."*

After that, we sat there for a while, both of us quiet. Until I couldn't stand the silence any longer and began to babble about why a life with Enrique was such a good idea. "He is the most kind and intelligent man I know," I said.

My father looked at me and took a pack of cigarettes and a box of matches from his pocket. "He is a goy, he doesn't understand our culture, our traditions," he said.

My voice was passionate, "Yes, he does, and we have the

---

6. Mishpucha in Yiddish literally means family, but in a general context means close friends that are like family, part of the "tribe."

same values, the same interests, we are best friends."

My father was a practical man and he started to ask practical questions. He asked where we would live; would he accept my religion? I said I wasn't religious, and Enrique wasn't either. And neither was my father, so why was he asking? Where, when would we get married? I said we hadn't thought that far yet.

When my father went back to Buenos Aires, I continued sending him almost daily letters, to keep him happy, to assuage my guilt at leaving him so alone. But also, to try to make him understand how I felt. I had been sending my father letters almost daily since he'd left me in the U.S. for the first time. But now I wrote to him obsessively, in my desire to convince him, to make him see my side. I was myself convinced that he was not just hurt, but also angry with me. I still have the letters where I told him that yes, it was definitive, Enrique and I would return home to marry before the end of the summer. Both of us were anxious and scared of what would happen when we finally made this decision a reality.

Six months after my father visited me in Maryland, we went back to Buenos Aires. Two weeks after our arrival, we were married in the afternoon by a Justice of the Peace; one of my oldest cousins and Enrique's sister acted as witnesses. Enrique was dressed in his usual dark suit, white shirt and thin dark tie. My father insisted that I should get an outfit made for the occasion, and a dressmaker we knew managed to design and sew in one week a perfect one, just for me. It had a jacket and a short skirt of a black and brown woven fabric; I wore it with a dark brown silk blouse with a big bow at the neck. In the picture we look elegant, stylish, our faces show bewilderment, we look somewhat disoriented and so very young!

We had been adamant that we didn't want a big party, no white dress nor any kind of pomp and circumstance. We considered any of that a waste of money we didn't have. And yet, there was a magical moment when in the afternoon, unrequested and unexpected, a box arrived at my door. Inside, there was an elegant knit white dress that fitted me to a T. It had a short skirt, long sleeves and it was gorgeous. The box the dress came in didn't say who had sent it and I could never find out who did, or how it could have been made or chosen to hang so well on my frame. These days I like to think that it was a miracle, even if those don't exist. It was a welcome gift because my father once again surprised us. He had planned for that evening a sixty-person wedding celebration at home. I wore the mysterious dress for the evening party, even if it was white.

My father was an amazing man. Although his job description was a boring "manager of an organization," the organization was the Association of Hotels, Confectioners, Restaurants and Cafes. He had only finished high school, but his work required him to discuss and negotiate the contracts between the owners of the various food related establishments and the work force. He started as a clerk and become a labor relations professional who was liked by both sides of the negotiation table. The job didn't pay well and was stressful, but it had its perks. He was on a first name basis with restaurant owners and chefs. Easter, Christmas and New Year, we received big baskets full of delightful goodies. We had the best rooms at the hotels for a discounted price. And of course, he could order, and get, the most striking cake, one that was unique for his only daughter's wedding party.

There was an even bigger surprise: all of my family and most of Enrique's family, as well as close friends, were there. The party was perfect. It was small enough, didn't have any pomp, and it gave us something to remember, a tale we told our kids many years later.

The day after the party, we left Buenos Aires and went back to Maryland to continue graduate school. Family members and friends were not too happy, but acquiesced, when we told them we couldn't accept objects as gifts because unless they were very small, it would be difficult and expensive to carry them with us to the States. That was in part true, but we also thought that we preferred to have money to buy ourselves in the States everything we wanted or needed. It was not something that was done at that time, and yet our families and friends came through with generous checks and cash that allowed us to furnish our empty apartment and save a bit in the bank.

In the end, my father became good friends with Enrique's parents. They shared for many years all of our letters home, called each other when they had news from us. I guess the moral of this story is that you can never predict what will happen, and we should question the rules we create for ourselves to live by. I was right to think that my choice would distress my father, but I was wrong that he would disapprove, that he would not support me as he had done all my life. I was also wrong about my family.

Enrique and I eventually immigrated to the United States. I believe that in the end, the stories of immigration, ours or others, are always stories of generosity, a desire of those who support us to sacrifice, to surrender, for the good of the loved ones.

Buenos Aires, 1969

Not Yet the End

We have reached the end, or a kind of end. Two of us, the N's will go from here to Madrid; two of us, Margaret and I, will continue to Finisterre, the end of the earth. And although no mystical revelations have come my way, I might have started on the path of a spiritual awakening…

I've conquered the fear of the unknown.
I've conquered the fear of being alone,
the fear of pain.
I've recovered some of the wonder
of so long ago
to reach this end,
this part of the story
where we raise our arms
and holler Victory!
before we fall off the cliff.

….

End and Beginning

Santiago, Spain

May 15, 2019

Certificate of Peregrination Completion, Camino Francés

Thoughts as We Reach the End

Today is the sixteenth day since we set off from Leon on El Camino de Santiago. We have reached our goal post. When I get up from my enormous bed in this palace of a hotel, and look at myself in the mirror, I can see on my face the past two weeks: the bright blue eyes that seem to contain the greens, the yellows, the purples of the trail; the small scar on my chin from when I fell on the trail; the lighter, longer, frizzy and messy hair, the mouth that smiles more often, opens in wonder. But I also see the other me, the young child, the teenager that never grew up, and the brave and shy woman, the mature me.

I think about how to describe us. These four women who have walked together, at this interval in their lives, so different in many ways, and so alike. We carry parts of each other, even if we wouldn't want to recognize that. We strive to be kind.

One has a well-defined taste for fashion and likes to dress up in yellows and oranges, chooses her accessories with care. A human machine marching single focus to her destination, she looks almost like a doll from behind. "I just go from point A to point B," she says. Where is the wonder in that, I ask? Oh, never mind.

Another walks with a stable purpose, carries her weight, which she dislikes, with flair and style. The wonder for her is how our bodies adjust. When we started, she had doubts that she could finish, she was in pain, but somehow her body responded, and she ended with joy, forgetting the pain.

The third one is a mother hen, tries to make peace where she finds disagreements. Argues both sides with calm. Until she can't, because she's in pain, her feet hurt, and she must use the energy to heal herself.

And then there is me, clueless about the rules of the social game, the outsider who just wants to play. The Jew among Christians, the blonde who grew up in the land of brunettes, the South American in North America.

But we all have engineers' brains, we analyze. We repress strong emotions, we adapt.

Today, we just rest and welcome our rewards. A leisurely, late breakfast — just the two of us, the M's — where we converse about how luscious, how luxurious these surroundings make us feel. Nelly has gone to mass, Nellie is socializing in town. After breakfast, Margaret and I go to get our certificates: the proof that we have walked this trail. I don't believe I need proofs to validate my accomplishments, but I still get them and keep them. Sometimes I even frame them. I think that they are an emotional reminder of the effort, of the journey. My college diploma was picked up by my father because when they gave it, I was in the States. My PhD diploma, I received in the mail. I didn't go to any of my graduations. Maybe this time, I want to celebrate not the end of another journey, but rather the beginning of a new awareness. The pleasure I get in conscious connection with other humans and with nature.

There is a long line of backpackers who have walked more than 100 kilometers of El Camino. 100 kilometers is the minimum you have to walk to get a certificate. The certificate shows how many kilometers you have walked. We walked at least 200 miles, more than 300 kilometers and feel, even if we try to hide it, a kind of superiority about that. Of course, the feeling lasts until we find hikers who have walked 600 kilometers, and thirty days or more to our puny sixteen — including two of "rest." In the end it doesn't matter how long we walked, how hard or easy it was, we all want to have this proof, this document of our trek, as if our memories or the pictures or whatever we might have learned were not enough.

All along our walk, we looked for the hotels, the cafés or restaurants that had "the El Camino stamp," and stopped in those places to get our El Camino passports stamped. It's proof that we have walked all the way and we need to show it to get our diploma of peregrines. I laugh. "This is so silly," I say, but still wait in line for mine. I tell myself that I only wait because the line goes fast. Later, I will frame my certificate and hang it on the wall behind my desk.

Afterwards, we sit with other walkers at a café. We sit around a round table, outside on the street, where we can see people stream by. We are seven or eight at the table, the number varies as some leave and others arrive. A couple of these men and women we have met at different times during the walk, others just drop by to say hi when they hear our chatting. I feel as if I have known all of them for a long time. There is our friend Daniel, the one who keeps the artistic journal and who we first met in Villafranca, and an English woman, Luisa, who Nellie and Margaret met going up O'Cebreiro. Luisa does Norwegian translations and knows almost everybody on El Camino. There are two young men who live in the U.S. but tease each other in Spanish. One was born in El Salvador and the other in Guatemala. It reminds me of the days, so long ago in Buenos Aires, when I sat drinking coffee from small cups and discussing the problems of the day. The cups here are small glasses instead, but the espresso is almost the same.

"This is good coffee," one of them says. His eyes are kind, and his demeanor is shy. His name is Tom, and he slouches and mumbles when he speaks. Tom is dressed in low-key browns, his friend, Juan, is louder, in color and sound. Juan wears a royal blue parka and matching hiking pants, and his voice carries to the next table. When he tastes his coffee and says:

"I like better the one we drink at home," the young woman sitting behind Tom, looks at Juan and nods with enthusiasm. I wonder if she's flirting, but then I notice that she is wearing a t-shirt with the Guatemalan colors. We all carry our home countries inside us.

"Oh, you Guatemalans," whispers Tom. "You've become a gourmet of the café." Then they start to discuss cultural differences in drinking coffee. I interrupt. I have heard this discussion too many times.

"How long have you walked? Is this your first time?" I ask. Luisa hears. "I hiked different parts of El Camino more than seven times," she says. Daniel has hiked in Japan, the UK, and who knows where else. Juan says with pride, "I walked El Camino three times," while Tom says that this is his first time. I think that at this table it's only Margaret and I, and the shy young guy, who have hiked only once. I stretch my eyebrows up in amazement when I hear their stories, and then ask myself if I would do it again. Oh, yes, I might, eventually, discover the art of the hike.

After a few coffees and, of course, a croissant, Margaret and I meander around with stupid smiles pasted on our faces and visit the interior of the cathedral. It's majestic and I admire the Romanesque architecture, the complex works of art. However, I'm not excited by its exuberance nor do I feel any particular emotion when I look into the many chapels, with their extravagantly decorated statues, or the paintings, retables, sculptures and reliquaries that have been accumulated with the passage of time. To me, this feels different from the outside architecture. Rather, I'm repelled by what to me just looks like a big bazaar of golden knick-knacks. And yet, I know, and understand, that to many people the inside of a church offers hope and serenity.

I wander around and take pictures of details that call my

attention. I notice a very long line of people slowly moving around a central semicircular area with many columns. The column statues represent the apostles, the prophets, and old Testament figures.

I choose a woman who holds the hand of a young girl by her side, wears a red headscarf and has a smile of adoration on her kind face to ask: "Why are you in line?" She looks at me as if I have landed from some alien planet.

"The middle pier represents Saint James," she says. "Are you a pilgrim?" I nod.

"Then you must touch the left foot of this statue to let it know that you have reached your destination." I thank her and move on. Why would I ever stand in line for hours to touch a foot of stone? One that so many hands have laid their hands on that they have worn a dirty groove on the stone. I don't want to be disrespectful, but internally I think that, although I was willing, barely, to wait in line for a piece of paper that certifies that I hiked 200 miles, I wouldn't be caught in a queue, not even a short one, just to let a stone statue know I finished my hike.

We meet with the N's, Nelly and Nellie, for a final lunch together.

"Is that a new type of purse?" I ask in fun when I see that Nellie's boots are knotted together by their shoelaces and she carries them, on her shoulder, like a bag.

"I want to give them to someone who needs them or leave them by the cathedral steps. I don't want to carry them back. I won't wear them again." she says.

I think it's sad, those boots walked with her so many miles. But then I notice that they are ruined. To let her feet breathe and expand, she cut the leather on the side of each boot. Each of us is leaving many things we no longer need behind. We lighten our bags and our minds, and then we weight them back with new stuff. I leave my fear, some of my grief and angst behind, and then I weight my heart with new friendships. It's a smart transaction.

We have lunch outside, at an Italian restaurant. We are tired of the same fare, but we can't resist the fresh tomatoes and other vegetables. We order salads. I also ask for the Vieira de mar, which the waiter tells me are scallops. It turns out to be a single big scallop immersed in tomato sauce over a big plastic shell. My friends laugh at the choice. It looks picturesque, but I'm afraid it might not be enough. However, there is sufficient bread, and it is delicious dipped in the scallop sauce. "I'm full," I say when I finish. "I'm happy," Nelly says, "My feet are happy inside my flip flops."

Afterwards we all go shopping together. I can feel the air of gaiety around us. A mantra inside our brains proclaiming, "We did it," again and again. We buy t-shirts with hiking themes and earrings of silver and black stone. Later in the afternoon we go back to the hotel and have a farewell cocktail with the N's, who are ready to leave, to get on their flight to Madrid.

In the evening Margaret and I stroll the cobblestone streets, looking for just the right place to eat. "Should we eat another omelet?" I say. Margaret laughs. "I think we have had enough eggs. But I'm not sure about the bread." We don't want anything heavy and walk around to find a small café that seems to have light faire. We sit, order salads with tuna and egg, and gossip about the day and our plans for the next. "Daniel is walking to Finisterre! It will take more than two days," Margaret says. "I prefer what we're doing. Some bus and some walking and we get there in just one day."

"I'm not as hike-focused crazy as Daniel," I say. "I want to enjoy some down time. Just walk in a leisurely way and absorb the landscape." And then, I turn around and there is Daniel sitting at a table behind us, eating dinner by himself. I look at Margaret and tell her in a whisper that I hope he doesn't hear well. "We didn't say anything bad, we were just talking about the day," Margaret says, and we laugh. When we finish, we go and say hi to Daniel who makes us believe he hadn't seen us sitting there.

Afterwards, we hear the music in the square and we dance, then we go back to the hotel to sleep.

Night of the Last Day in Santiago

I have questions but no answers. Have I changed with this experience? Do I have less fear, am I more gentle, stronger, what? My skin is definitely drier and darker. My thighs are stronger, and the bottoms of my feet are harder; I still take my vitamins, do yoga at night, worry about my kids, my house, what to expect of life. I'm still me, with images in my mind, of this and other trips and of the trips to come. I have memories, photographs and plans for a lifetime. The gate in my emotional fence has been left open. I wonder if my feelings will escape.

Tomorrow, Margaret and I will go to Finisterre and, as I fall asleep, I reminisce. I have this album of moments, colored pictures, inside my head. The day we stood atop the Acropolis, when it was still allowed; the day I couldn't breathe at the sight of the Duomo in Florence, when I said, "We made it. We have arrived," because I felt, what else was to see after that? I didn't understand we were already leaving, and there was so much more, that time would start to go faster and faster. The tape in my head runs back and forth. I think of the view of the New York Hudson, and New York City, from the plane, a naïve 19-year-old, my father next to me. The view of the Manhattan skyline so many years later, when my husband and I drove through on our way north to attend the college graduation of our first son. The infinite drives. I see our car and the kids, at six and 10, traveling through the South of France, and later traveling with teens through Italy, Cinque Terra, my oldest son with a jar of pesto that he cared for as if it were a baby he was carrying, all the way back to L.A. I see my husband and I, a young couple, driving the roads of the former Yugoslavia,

Bosnia and Herzegovina today. A harrowing drive around the mountains, under pouring rain, my husband at the wheel, in our smashed, rented bright yellow Passat, sticking out like a yellow post among all the Soviet-era black cars. The flowers around the corners on the worst curves. "*Curva pericuolosa,*" we'd scream, and laugh, me scared shitless, as if we were on an amusement park ride. These were the places where a car had fallen off the cliff. The flowers a memorial or an alert, the sign for a dangerous curve, "*Curva pericuolosa!*" A jumble of moments. The drive through Hungary, trying to reach Romania before nightfall. Oh, yes, Hungary. Didn't the fall I took in Molinaseca remind me of that day?

A Lucky Collision – Hungary, 1974

I wake up inside the car; the car is not upright. It is lying on its side in a ditch, and I'm stuck against the passenger door, which can't be opened. My husband, at my side, says "Oh, shit!" He never curses in English. "The cart, that guy didn't have a light." And I know it could be bad.

"What cart?" I say, trying to unfasten the seat belt and turn around. "I swerved to avoid it, but I saw it too late, he didn't have a light, I banged its side," he says. And then I hear the panic in his voice. "The guy, did I hurt the guy?" I look outside, but it's still dark, we have been driving all night. He opens his door, it still works, and gets out. I hop over the manual gearshift to the other side of the car and follow. We're in the middle of a field with nothing in sight. Just the narrow road, the grass on the other side. We don't see the cart, or the horse, or the driver, but our car, in the ditch, is smashed on the passenger side.

"How can they let cars and carts on the same road! He didn't have a light. I couldn't stop." My husband takes pride in his driving. I know he can't process, yet, what's happened. He is an excellent driver. Still, we're spooked but fine. We both have all our body parts, and nothing hurts. We are lucky.

"I think the cart driver was more scared than we were and didn't want to stay. He must be OK," I try to comfort him. After all, this is Hungary. I wonder if maybe he could get arrested for driving a horse-pulled cart without lights.

It was 1974, still the Cold War days, and we'd rented the car in Vienna. They gave us a beautiful car, a new, shiny yellow, manual transmission Passat. The plan was to drive down through Hungary, where we could get a two-day visa, then continue through Romania, check out a place near where my ancestors came from, and then go on to Yugoslavia and up to Trieste, Italy, and back to Vienna where we would return the car. Thus, our first stop was Hungary.

In Hungary, we visited friends of our friends (who were Hungarian). We thought that we would be invited to stay the night there. But they didn't invite us to stay; their apartment was too small, or, during those times, they might have been afraid of hosting foreigners, even if friends of friends.

At 10 p.m., we realized we had to leave and find somewhere to stay for the night. But we were graduate students, traveling on five dollars a day, and couldn't afford expensive hotels. We looked around and the cheap lodgings didn't have any vacancies. We drove to the bus station; in other countries that's where we usually found lodging information. At the door, a large woman looked at us and in a mix of German, Hungarian and English, she said, "Zimmer, come, come, zimmer, five dollars." She had a room (zimmer) for five dollars and we said OK. We drove her to her house, but when we got there, the zimmer was just her own room, we would sleep in her bed. We left in a hurry when she showed that she would sleep on the floor, next to us. We felt bad about the poor woman, but also paranoid about what kind of scam she could be running. We decided it would be safer to just drive and sleep along the way. The urgency was because we had a visa for only two days. We'd already been one day and some hours in Hungary.

Now, as we look around, trying to figure out what to do, how to get the car out of the ditch, suddenly, as if by magic, people, peasants, start to appear from the field. They look at us, but we can't communicate. They don't speak English; we don't speak Hungarian. I'm afraid they might want to attack us, we're foreigners after all. We make gestures, how to get the car upright, see if it will drive. Nothing. Then, there is a young guy, who tries languages with us. Magyar? No. Ross-SEE-sky? Nyet (my husband studied some Russian but can't speak it). Then we ask: English? No Spanish? No French, Italian? No, nyet. German? The young guy asks. My husband shakes his head, "Nein." "Wait," I say, I think in desperation, maybe we can understand German, maybe. We studied German together for a year or so, a while back, maybe something stuck. I nod, we'll try. The guy says "Polizei?" and I fret. Does he want to take us to the police? But he talks and gestures and, to my amazement, I understand, I answer back. He is young and strong and between the three of us, while the whole town watches, we push and lift the car out of the ditch. It starts and everyone applauds. Everybody is in good spirits. Except us, we sigh with relief. We thought we would be hanged right there, but no.

The guy — who we now think of as "our guide," and then we learn his name is George, although it could be anything that sounds like that — knows someone who could get the car fixed so that we can drive out of town in time. George leads the way on his motorcycle, and we follow behind. My husband performs miracles by letting the car slide and go in first gear so it can reach this shack where an elderly couple, farmers, receives us, and with gestures, nods and smiles, they try to reassure us. We feel dubious, but without another option, we leave them the car, with our luggage in the trunk.

George says they will fix it so we can drive, and then he signals for us to mount behind him, squeezed next to each other, on his motorbike, so he can take us to the police station nearby. The station opens at 10 a.m., but it is 8 a.m. and we wait. Our guide with us. We tell him that we are worried, we have to get out before early afternoon, or they will stop us at the border. He says it will be OK. When two policemen arrive, George leaves, he should have been at work, but stayed to help us. We were the highlight of his day.

Then, time starts to pass. First slowly, then quickly. But during those several hours while we wait, anxious and worried, to see if we can get the car and drive across the border, get to Romania before our Hungarian visa is no longer valid, the two policemen distract and entertain us. I don't know if they want to make us feel better, or we are an entertainment for them, with so few foreigners around. It is fascinating, in hindsight, to realize that we discussed, without knowledge of each other's languages, just using the few words we knew in German and lots of gestures: the politics of Argentina, how to dance tango, the particulars of the car we were driving, and then they taught us how to count in Hungarian. I still remember how.

Two hours before our visa expires, one of them takes us to our car. It still has a bump on the passenger side, that door will not open, and I have to enter through the driver side, but the car now runs well. The man and woman, a couple of farmers in my mind, knew how to fix a German car, would not accept any payment, so we take a picture of them by their small house, really a small barn. We are so grateful that I want to kiss the farmers and the policemen. My face hurts from how long I smile.

People can communicate if they really want to. In the end, we are all the same. I have lost the picture of the farmers, but it is engraved in my memory. The man next to his wife in front of their door. He wears a blue overall, she a yellow dress with flowers, her hands on her stomach, his on her arm. On each of their faces, a shy smile. It comes back in moments like this, when one journey is about to end, and another begins.

And then we drive, in a smashed new yellow Passat; a car in which I can't open the passenger door and must hop to the other side to get out. We make it to the border in time and *then keep driving this car, all through countries behind the iron curtain, among all black cars. We are stopped at the gates of each town and asked to explain where, how did we crash? Why is the passenger door smashed? But they let us pass. It must show on our faces that we still have a long journey ahead.*

245

Ashes to the Sea

Finisterre, Spain

May 16, 2019

Walk down to the Cruceiro

A Meal With Strangers

On our way to the Finisterre, *fin de la tierra*, the end of the earth, I find myself sitting down to lunch, at the end of a long table, sharing a meal with twenty-three strangers.

That morning, Margaret and I had taken a bus to go to *Kilometer Zero* (Finisterre). The idea was to stop at the main sights between Santiago and "the end" — at the ocean — do small hikes along the way and then wander around once we got there. This hike-and-ride option was our compromise with time and emotion. We didn't have two days to hike another eighty kilometers, and we also felt, once we'd gotten to Santiago, that we were "done."

However, as soon as we boarded the bus, even though the day was cold and rainy, we felt full of adrenaline, looking forward to one more adventure. We had our rain gear, the stuff we had been lugging all this time and, fortunately, only had to use only a few times. This would be the last part of our journey, the icing on the cake.

The bus had stopped at our hotel to pick up the two of us and a couple of other passengers. Then it stopped a few more times until there were twenty-five of us. We would all ride and walk or hike together on our way to Finisterre. The bus passed through farming towns, and we learned that, in Galicia, 350,000 cows are milked each day, that each cow consumes 60 liters of water and 50 kilos of food and produces 25 liters of milk. I'll only drink soy milk, I thought; all these cows are good for Galicia's economy, but bad for the earth.

The bus crossed a bridge (Ponte Maceira) and the driver stopped so we could walk by the Tambre River. There was a cascade and two old water mills, probably from the 1600s. I walked over a small bridge and stepped inside one of the mills. It still contained the large grinding stones, and it smelled of flour. Or so I imagined, as I imagined the paddle wheel attached to a shaft, attached to a runner stone, and the water rushing to turn one large circular stone against the other to grind the meal between them.

The path around the mills was uneven, and there was the possibility of falling into the river. So, I stepped gingerly to take pictures of how the water reflected the sun, flowed between stones, and cascaded. It left a postcard in my mind.

We rode the bus another while, taking breaks to walk or hike around a few other sights, a Mirador, more waterfalls, a hydroelectric power plant. There was a small cart where a woman was selling tchotchkes and I couldn't resist buying a couple of bracelets and some earrings. "They are for gifts," I said by way of justification. "For my homies and my housekeeper." Although I might wear the earrings myself.

When we were almost at Finisterre, but not quite, we were starving, the bus stopped and we stepped out. It was our break for lunch. There was a picturesque harbor full of colorful boats, and we walked along the waterfront to a restaurant. The scenic landscape made us slow down our walking, even though we were hungry and thinking about food.

Now, at the restaurant, there is a long table that has been reserved for all of us who are doing this ride/walk together from Santiago. This is how I find myself sitting with Margaret near the end of a long table and observing the twenty-three strangers who will share the meal with us. They have all hiked all or part of El Camino and I ask where they come from. New Zealand, Croatia, a couple from Korea, a young guy from Brazil. A group of three women from Mexico sitting next to us say, "We have only hiked three days. We were afraid we wouldn't last."

"No matter," we reply, "we are all peregrines, each of us in their own way."

There is a single woman from Nigeria, a couple from Costa Rica, a woman from France, a few guys from Spain — Andalucía, Zaragoza — an athlete from Canada, a woman sitting next to me, over 80 years old, from Wales. She says, "I'm getting old, I hike slower now, take my time." (Later, when we hike amid rocks, with a strong wind in our faces and the ocean at our feet, I'm amazed to see her tread between the boulders, walk under the coastal rocks, ocean water sloshing her boots, with a sure footing that I don't have the balance or the courage to attempt.)

And then, there's the two of us from L.A.: an American of Lebanese descent, and an American born in Argentina of Rumanian, Russian, German/Hungarian/Austrian — and who knows what else? — descent.

After the appetizer, a tuna stuffed *empanada Gallega*, we are no longer strangers, we share our stories, our failures and our successes. The woman from Nigeria talks about the isolation she felt part of the way; the Mexicans next to us wish they could have had the courage to hike for a week. They look at us in awe when we tell them we started more than two weeks ago in Leon. But then we hear from the Canadian woman, who has walked all the way from Saint-Jean-Pied-de-Port, on the French side of the Pyrenees, in twenty-five days.

"What?" I say, "That is not possible."

"When I started, there was still snow on the path, and I had to go slower," she tells us matter-of-factly, to explain why it took her more than twenty days.

"You didn't walk, you ran," I say, and she smiles.

"Most days I did 40-kilometers, but I run iron man competitions, in the mountains in Canada. I'm used to hiking during very cold weather and on high paths. It's what I do."

She is a real athlete who trains every day, but she's a normal looking, slender woman. We notice that she seems lonely, as if she is looking for company.

Then, there is the French woman, who also travels alone and talks about her struggle with her feet to make it to the end. The Brazilian guy is the youngest of us; he makes us laugh with his jokes. The couple from South Korea seemed aloof when they got onto the bus, and now they are too far down the table for me to hear what they say. However, I can't avoid staring when I notice their connection with the Italians sitting next to them. I laugh, we are the peregrines of the United Nations. There should be a requirement that all the members of the U.N. go on an El Camino hike together.

At the end of the meal, we all walk for a while under a drizzle around the harbor and then finally board the bus for the last stretch to reach Finisterre. We are excited to make it to the end of this long journey, but I have seen so much, walked so many paths, already, that I think now I'm really done, that the feeling of awesome, amazing or surprising experiences has expired.

But of course, on this journey, as on any, there is always an unexpected turn. Once we stop and I get off the bus, step onto the waterfront promenade and get my first glance of the cape, I'm mesmerized. There is a rough, jagged and treacherous, bright and intense looking coastline. A slope of slippery boulders and rocks leads to a cross, or *Cruceiro*, near the breaking water. The cross stands on a large round boulder and I watch how a few people tread their way there and bend over and seem to deposit something at its base, in a kind of ritual, maybe in gratitude that this part of the journey is over.

The locket, with some of Enrique's ashes inside, has been throbbing on my chest all this time. The small and by now scrunched up piece of paper, with its scribbled list of names, has been nudging my hand each time I touch my pocket. I wrote the names on a page I tore from a small spiral notebook before I left home and have been transferring the crumpled piece of paper from pants-pocket to pants-pocket as I start each day. It's an act of defiance against the tangible world, a wish that those who were not with me, who couldn't be, would travel with me, anyway, to the end.

There is this dichotomy between magic and the laws of physics that I sometimes struggle with inside my brain. On the paper, I wrote Enrique's name, and I wrote the name of Mónica, my cousin and best friend when we were young, who died in a car accident at thirty-six years of age, and my dead parents' names, and I wrote the names of two of my best and most supportive friends who are well and alive, but stayed home and, from afar, wish me well. This is the place where I will leave the dead and invoke the spirits of those I love, at the end of the earth, although my journey will never end.

I start to walk down the slope to the cross, over the boulders, and my step is careful but firm. There is a strong wind, the boulders are high; it would be easy for me to trip. Margaret watches me from above and frets. She guards me with her eyes, hoping that will keep me safe. "I can't come and help you if you fall," she yells. "I promised my family I would stay safe."

Me? I only promised to have courage and to be kind, to everybody and to myself. So, I go slowly, but I go. I remember the dream I had after my long walk of preparation on the Strand, when I put my locket around my neck. Now, when I reach the last boulder, next to the large cross, I take the paper from my pocket, tear the lined page into small pieces and throw them with a bit of the ashes from my locket to the sea.

I climb back up the boulders, my locket with the remaining ashes around my neck. Margaret breathes of sigh of relief that I'm back all in one piece, and then we walk to the post that says "0.00 Kilometers." We ask another hiker to take our picture, with our thumbs up and, under the hoods of our raincoats, huge smiles. Then, of course, I buy a blue and yellow t-shirt that says, "km 0."

The Blooms of the Bougainvillea

Sometimes I have to laugh at myself. How I manage the two opposite sides of my brain. A superstitious scientist doesn't make sense. And yet, some days, some years, while I defend facts, calculate complex mathematical equations, I also quiz the source of my mystical beliefs. I spread cremation ashes on the soil, on the sand and the ocean; I look for signs. I find an old soul within the pupils of a dog's eyes. I talk to the trees and the flowers along my way and wonder if dreams are part of another reality. I don't think that to soar with nature is superstitious, but rather a component of my being. Carl Sagan said it well: "Science is not only compatible with spirituality; it is a profound source of spirituality.... When we grasp the intricacy, beauty, and subtlety of life, then that soaring feeling, that sense of elation and humility combined, is surely spiritual... The notion that science and spirituality are somehow mutually exclusive does a disservice to both."[7]

And then, there is this: how to make a life story out of the shards of memory?

2005 – The bougainvillea, my precious Santa Rita, didn't bloom that spring. I missed its red paper-thin flowers giving color to the white stucco walls at the front of our house. It was the spring we came back from the doctor with a diagnosis of lung cancer for my husband. Stage 4, a death sentence. The next morning, a Sunday, I prepared brunch while my tears turned

---

7. Carl Sagan – The Demon-Haunted World: Science as a Candle in the Dark

pink as they slid and slithered over the fresh red strawber-ries I was slicing into small pieces. We ate in silence, then we discussed options. Surgery was not one of them. Chemo and radiation had been offered with a moderate probability of cure.

We sat together at the computer and studied the five-year predicted survival curve. It didn't look good, but neither did the alternative. The decision was to go with chemo once a week, radiation every day except weekends. Every week we practiced denial, but I couldn't stomach the sight of the needle punctur-ing the vein, the red blood coming out.

Soon, fatigue set in, and he had to use a cane. His legs be-came sticks that wouldn't hold his thin frame. At the front of the house, the leaves of the bougainvillea had ragged edges. The plant was dying, being eaten by small, invisible bugs. I spread poison all over its leaves, fertilized the soil. The leaves turned the color of rust.

At the end of the summer, I saw a green leaf on the withered Santa Rita. Superstition set in. If the plant survives, if it revives and turns green and blooms red again, so will my husband, I said to myself, aware that I had become irrational.

Fall came, the tumor and the fatigue receded. The bou-gainvillea was green. It sprouted red flowers at the end of the following spring. At the end of the next summer my husband and I crossed Paris, walking, from east to west. About 10 kilo-meters, a red paper flower in my hair.

The Way Back to Santiago

It could have been a letdown, after this climax, to ride back to the hotel on this bus, but it isn't. As I watch the sights go by in reverse, the images from today, and of many other days, are on repeat in my brain while I listen, as if to welcome music, to the chatting and stories of my fellow travelers all around me.

It is late evening, and a holiday weekend, the streets around the historical square are closed to cars and buses. The driver offers to some of us who are staying at the Parador to leave us within a couple of blocks of the hotel, but we ask to be let off before that, when we are still about a mile away. We prefer to walk while our thoughts whirl inside our heads.

I later learn that the streets are closed in preparation for the next day's festival, *el Día de las Letras Gallegas*, the Galician Literature Day. A day that includes conferences and readings, but also, like most Spanish festivals, it is full of music and dance. As we near the square, we can hear the sound of bagpipes. The Canadian athlete is walking back with us. We think that after her long trek by herself, she is in need of human companionship. We are mesmerized by her tales of long hikes at high altitudes, with snow and ice, even more so because she seems so normal otherwise, so average. She is slight, and limber, but her body doesn't look extra-muscular or hard. When we show our admiration, she tells us about her friend who does the whole Camino in two weeks. "Really?!" It took us two weeks to do 200 miles. How do you do 400 miles in the same amount of time? Does she have superpowers, we ask. "That's just what she does," our Canadian friend says, and we detect a twinge of jealousy in her voice.

Another Last Time

Because this is near the end of this adventure, because I could climb up and down without aid over slippery boulders, when I sat on the bus that was taking us back to the hotel, I closed my eyes and watched as in a dream another last trip, another climb, another ending.

There is the before and the after, and the days near the end. In the end, he, my husband, my best friend, passed away.

The "before" is before the diagnosis, all those journeys of discovery we took together, the long walks, the thousands of photographs in black and white, and later, color slides and finally, digital — but of these last, not so many. The "after" is after the diagnosis, the journeys to make memories, the joy of traveling together one more time, and still the many photographs. Now all digital. The end is the last trip together, and then the last month.

When I take a shower, it turns on; when I brush my teeth, it becomes loud; and when, at home, I take out the trash, the guilt piles up and then I laugh, a sad laugh because I no longer have someone to laugh with or to laugh at. The kids and I used to tease him about his obsession with gathering every single piece of trash from our rooms, depositing it in the big trash cans and rolling them to the street the day before trash pickup time. I'd say, "Why do you stress about it? It's not so critical if we're left with some trash for next week."

He would take it in stride: "It will overflow otherwise."

Now, when I'm home, I have to do it by myself, and I do the same thing he did.

The images from the shower, or brushing my teeth, are different, they are from the last month, near the end, his end, and they tear at my gut. He had trouble with his hands, the soap would slip, he couldn't hold the toothbrush and needed my help.

The question comes and goes, and then stays. How do I quiet a memory, that tape that goes on and on, when there is no button, no parallel bars to click and stop the reel, to lower the sound that today is so damn loud? The end of a journey, of an adventure, triggers the pain, and the pleasure, of these recollections.

Jamaica – June 2014. The last trip we took together, five years ago, was ten years after the diagnosis, and a lifetime ago. We flew to Jamaica in the middle of summer. The day we left, he looked frail, too thin, after a late winter bout of pneumonia, and yet he had his backpack on his shoulders, held his small carry-on with one hand and held our passports in his other hand when he turned his head to me and smiled. To be able to travel meant there was a future. Maybe, I thought, we have another ten years. I'm good at denial, I have had lots of practice.

In his backpack he carried his prized Nikon camera and telephoto lens and the iPad he only used to play Sudoku. Other times, there had been two or three cameras, multiple lenses. But this time, his backpack was lighter and so, I thought, was the trip.

I had planned something different than our usual travel: this time we would just take a trip to a destination, two weeks stay at an all-inclusive resort. No long walks on uneven city streets, no trains, just a couple of flights. But I couldn't find direct flights to Montego Bay. I used miles to upgrade the longest leg, a four-hour flight, to first class.

How could I have been so naïve, or so blind? That simple trip was hard for him, and even with so much practice it was hard for me to avoid reality. The resort was amazing, right on the beach. A couple of pools, lounge chairs overlooking the ocean, free cocktails, massages, you name it. But I hadn't counted on the stairs, and the steps up and down, and his recent muscle weakness, legs that didn't respond as before, a brain that didn't provide enough balance.

As soon as we arrived, I should have seen my mistake, but I didn't want to see. Sometimes I prefer to remain blind to painful realities. A pleasant young woman, one of the front desk clerks, came over to greet us and give us a tour of the premises. "The bus boy will carry your luggage to your room while I show you the resort; and afterwards you may want to have a cocktail, or two, on the terrace," she said.

"Great," I said. But he remained quiet, a look of discontent on his face. I was annoyed, here we were in paradise and he didn't seem to appreciate it. I don't remember exactly what I said, but it wasn't nice. Something like, "Oh, you never want to explore."

The day was gray, threatening rain. The young woman walked with a firm step ahead of us towards a staircase. It was the only way to go from the lobby, on the first floor, down to the beach below, and also, it turned out, to our rooms. There was no elevator. Thus, each time we wanted to enter or leave the hotel, or spend time in the lobby, or check the gift shop, we would have to use this staircase. It was a curved staircase, with at least thirty steep steps that became narrower at the turns. And yet, he made the effort, held on to the rail, went down, looked at the armchairs set up for happy hour, at the beach. Our rooms were about one hundred feet away.

Then the clerk kept walking, further down, more steps towards the sand. She said she wanted to show us other buildings nearby. He said, "No." He didn't want to see anymore. He would wait for me in the room, or just stand there. I insisted.

"Look, afterwards we can have a cocktail there," I pointed to the comfortable loungers overlooking the ocean. I didn't see, I didn't want to see, what he saw: an obstacle course where each step would require effort and the high probability of tripping or falling. He didn't move, and I gave up. The clerk understood. She looked at me and said: "I'll give you the short tour while he waits. It looks like it's going to rain anyway."

I took the short tour, to find out where everything was, under a drizzle that soon became a light rain. I was sad, this was supposed to be our vacation, not just mine. I wanted to have a cocktail, dance under the stars. Instead, I went back to the room, put our clothes away, changed, and then we walked out for dinner.

The path to the restaurants — there were at least two of them — was flat, easy to negotiate; the many food options and the free cocktails raised both of our spirits. He was happy, and so was I. I always adapt, try to see the good side. I don't like to feel gloomy or depressed. And so it was that, although we couldn't walk up and down the beach, climb up and down the stairs, dance the night away, we could enjoy the food, the music, and the hammocks next to the ocean. A couple of times he even walked to the ocean and lay there on his back, lulled by the soft waves, the warm breeze. One day we had a couple's massage. Something he would never have done in a different set up. Another day we took a tour in a van. We had to go up the staircase and I could see how hard it was for him, that single story climb. He, who only ten years ago could carry our grown-up children on his back up the stairs of our house.

One morning, after we had been there a week, he lost his balance in the bathroom, fell against the marble floor. I still don't know how he didn't break anything, or maybe he did; maybe he broke his will to live.

I knew something was wrong when a few days later, he woke up in the middle of the night with a pain in his shoulder. He never woke up in the middle of the night. Not even when he had had a bad cough. He loved to sleep.

And yet, and yet, I could still deny. When we went to tour the main Kingston sights, he got out of the van to watch the people dive into the water from a very high cliff; he even took their pictures. We bought t-shirts that said "Rick's Café." But he didn't want to walk, he sat on a stone bench, his face pale. One afternoon I convinced him to go to the pool, get in the water. We ate as much cheese and drank as many cocktails as our bodies allowed. The resort gave us a cake on the day of our 45th anniversary to celebrate. We even watched Argentina's soccer team on the resort TV, and he cheered when the team won a place in the World Cup semifinals.

And when the last day came, we went up the curved staircase one last time. We got to the airport. Flew the first leg. He was tired. I said, "It is OK, next leg is first class." But the wait at the Charlotte airport was long. The gate was changed three times, from one end to the other end of the terminal. The third time he refused to walk, we called the people mover, but it wouldn't arrive on time and we had to walk and walk fast so we wouldn't miss the plane. I kept thinking, it is going to be OK, we have first class, he can rest when we get to our seats. But when I looked at him, his eyes were unfocused, he seemed to be in another world, and for the first time I was afraid. I walked in front, carrying both carry-ons and both backpacks. He followed me as in a daze. We made it, and we sat in our first-class seats, but I knew then, even if I didn't want to say it to myself: This is the beginning of the end.

And yet… the day after we got home, he wore his Argentina T-shirt, and we watched the final game of the World Cup. I thought, "Maybe we have a reprieve," even though Argentina lost. We had a reprieve, we had eight more months. And I will always wonder if anything would have been different if we had not traveled that last time, if he had not fallen at the hotel in Jamaica and maybe broken something unseen inside?

I Am

I am a bell sounding in the rain,
I am the blue jay in the path,
picking at the seeds covered with lavender.
I am the soil, where we dropped your ashes,
so white they looked like sand.

I am the wide river, made of silver.
I am the bottle of Malbec we shared
on our last trip,
when we went to Jamaica,
that day we celebrated,
our 45th wedding anniversary.

I am The Thinker, the Rodin sculpture we saw in Paris
after we had walked six miles,
you with a child on your shoulders.

I am the sculpture of Aphrodite
standing naked, Mother Goddess
we stared at in awe
at the Aphrodisias Museum
in Turkey,
and the tea we sipped
in the caves with
the free people, the noble men
from the Atlas Mountains of Morocco,
still dizzy after all the turns in mountain roads.

I'm the *dulce de leche* you still loved to taste
when there wasn't, any longer,
a food you could eat.

I am all our journeys,
I carry you.
I wear my beret
I hold your hand in mine.

This Is Not the END

Santiago to Madrid, Spain

May 17, 2019

Kilometer 0.0

The Way to Madrid

Today, after we pack, we meet for breakfast. A relaxed one that includes lots of coffee, yogurt, and bread. "Let's go for our last walk to the square," I tell Margaret. Once we are out, we gaze one last time at the view of the wondrous cathedral, the Romanesque structure with gothic and Baroque additions that I don't get tired of photographing. There are people lying on the worn-down flagstones, cameras or iPhones in their hands, trying to get the right selfie with the cathedral in the background for their Instagram posts. I guess I'm not the only one who's mesmerized by this majestic site. When I point out to Margaret the guy lying on his side who is moving around like a contortionist to fit his girlfriend and the top of the church in the same frame, we both laugh.

We stride around, hear music and watch with fascination the large groups of Galicians, young, old and very old, who come up the side streets towards the square and start to dance. They move forward and back, up and down, alone or in pairs, fast and with grace, an intense joy on their faces, to the sounds of the bagpipes that can be heard from afar.

I get fixated on their costumes, which date from the 19th century. The women cover their heads and shoulders with short or long shawls, *mantillas*. They wear long red and black wool skirts; the fabric takes one and a half turns around their hips. An apron, black, white or red is tied at the waist above the skirt. I stare, open mouthed, at an older woman who is dancing with zest next to me.

It's so hot, I think, and yet she has so much joy, moving and jumping and wearing that heavy costume. When she turns around, I take a picture and admire the piece of cloth folded in a triangular shape and adorned with velvet and rhinestones that she wears on her back. Its two ends pass around and cross on her chest and then go back and tie again at the back. She notices my stare and tells me: "It is called dengue." I wonder how that piece of clothing got the name of a mosquito that brings a bad disease.

The men have triangular hats on their heads, short jackets made of wool, hose that go from their knees to their feet. Everything has lots of fine and delicately embroidered lace, and the velvet is inlaid with precious stones and glitter. On their feet, they wear clogs made of leather with wooden soles. When I see the older woman dancing along with a young man, I want to join them, dance and jump with them. And I do, while I take pictures, so that many of my photos will end up blurred. When I look at them afterwards, I think they have the right feeling after all.

In the early afternoon, we take a taxi to the Santiago de Compostela airport, and in less than two hours we are in a different world — a sterile, modern hotel near the Madrid Barajas airport. We had made the decision to sleep at a hotel near the airport this last night in Spain before our flight to Los Angeles. This way, we won't have to hurry in the morning to take our long flight back home. But we also don't have much to do in the evening. "What do we do now?" we ask each other.

The streets around the hotel are dull, free of any interest or charm. "Let's just stay in the hotel and meditate until dinner, then eat at the hotel restaurant," says Margaret. When we come down and sit at one of the restaurant tables — also lacking charm — I say to Margaret; "What a difference from the small towns and the Parador." I check the menu to see if it is as drab as the restaurant. But of course, this is Spain. "Lots of tasty food to choose from," I say. But then, each of us orders only a salad. It turns out to be one of the best, with tuna fish and hard-boiled egg and olives and a few walnuts, just in case.

As we eat, we talk, trying to move our minds toward the world ahead, while we also reminisce about the world we are leaving behind. "I think that my husband will be waiting for us when we arrive at LAX," Margaret says. "I hope that the flight is not too crowded, and I can sleep," I say, "and that we don't have to wait too long for our bags."

As many times as I travel, and most of the time these days I travel alone, I find it difficult to transition between one place and the next. At night, to soothe my inner turmoil before going to sleep, I write.

The next day, when we get up, our minds are already on Los Angeles time.

Perpetual Traveler

My brain is en route to Paris,
while my body is in Madrid,
but my feet still walk the *Camino* trail,
and my dreams are full of green.

Images of tilled fields,
songs of cuckoo-birds,
a rooster's crow,
the sheep's bleating.

The smell of herbs, wine,
olives and manure
mixed in the breeze.

Next to my bed,
my boots tell the stories,
while I fall asleep.

A Prayer from an Areligious Jew

Long let me walk these old cobblestone streets, avoid tripping on the uneven pavement; keep my bones strong as I wander, travel, stroll, another round around this world. Let me hear the blaring of the horns and the screech of the skateboards, the sirens of the ambulances, the hip-hop beats coming through the open windows, the conversations in the cafés and the songs of the birds. Let me smell the sweetness of the eggs, flour and sugar as they become a delicious crepe, the Lily of the Valley, the Hyacinth in bloom.

Long let me have this zest for life, this hunger, this appetite, that lets me keep grief and sorrow at bay, keep alive a love for human friends, animals, nature, technology and the unknown.

If you could know all that I still want to live. I want to touch the texture of the concrete walls, see the Banksys, the graffiti, the shows at the Atelier de la Lumiere. I want to hold again a baby in my arms, caress the black fur of a small dog, cuddle next to my sons, dance, experience a new love and, while I live all of that, keep all the memories of you.

CODA

Afterlife: After I die

In the afterlife I won't exist, but I'll be alive. Alive in the grass beside the wooden stairs that lead to the beach. Alive in the seeds of the agrimony and anise root plants that grow wild in the soil beneath the trees along the path. Alive in the sand that is swept by the wind to the steely ocean and then comes back. Alive as you are. When I die, I won't exist, but I want to be alive in the streets where I grew up. I want my ashes to be strewn in the same old places where yours are.

I want a brass band to parade by my house, to play Latin music, salsa, bachata, and for everyone to come out and dance. In the afterlife I won't exist, but I want my story to be read, to be kept alive.

When I die, I ask that my ashes be mixed with yours inside the two small silver lockets I bought on Amazon.com as a lark. And on the Day of the Dead, I want my sons to build an altar. And I will come back. I will wear ten *chaquiras* bead bracelets, all hues of blue and green, yellow and orange, on each arm. I will wear bright white blouses, embroidered with *Colibris* sucking marigolds in the colors of the rainbow, shiny red and turquoise sandals, long plaid skirts and a green scarf. I will wear purple painted acrylic earrings and a black cape with red stripes. I know, I know, none of these colors go well together, but friends, this would be the afterlife and I would be alive. Alive in the memories, I hope, of those who I love, as you are in mine.

May 2019

Acknowledgments

I am grateful and indebted to my writer's community, my squad of friends and my dear family who motivated me, supported me, and accepted my quirks during this long unplanned but welcomed journey. In particular, I would like to express my profound thanks to:

Cecilia Woloch, who many years ago provided the pivotal feedback to unveil a voice I didn't know I had. She was the one who said I could write a book instead of keeping my journal in a drawer and my many essays in a computer folder. She also had the patience to edit and re-edit the many drafts of this book.

My walking companions, the ones who walk with me almost every week and who were next to me during the long hikes of *El Camino de Santiago*. Without them I wouldn't have started or completed this fascinating hiking adventure. Gals, you rock!

The many teachers and workshop leaders who guided me along the way. Jessica Barksdale, Carolyn Levitt, Laura Davis, Vanessa Poster, are just a few who were either at the beginning or near the end of my learning curve (but this curve has no end). Although the list is too extensive to mention each of them by name, their words of wisdom and feedback are etched in my brain.

The writers at the many writer groups I attended during this transformative journey. I want to single out Kris Anderson and Jan Hanson for giving the best advice and inviting me to their poetry group. I want to thank as well the Manhattan Beach Poetry Circle, in particular Bob Perkins, Elaine Mintzer and Peggy Carter who always give constructive advice on my poems and listen with kindness to my first unrefined drafts. A high five to Carmen Palmer who cheered me on via Zoom from Puerto Rico as I completed the last stretch of the book proofs. A special shout-out to the Venice writer's group, the first writer's group I ever attended, where I made friendships that remain to this day.

My Atmosphere Press editor Tammy Letherer and my proof-readers, Hannah Lamb-Vines and Chris Beale: you are the best.

And last, but foremost in my heart and mind:

My sons who had to deal with a scientist-turned-writer mom and who were kind enough to read drafts of this book, offer advice on the cover, support my readings, correct my grammar and my accent. I love you both. You are my pillars of strength.

And more than thanks, my whole self, goes to my best friend and companion of 50 years. The one who watched me begin my transition from scientist to writer and supported me all the way. This first book is dedicated to you, Enrique. I miss you every day.

About the Author

MARIA CAPONI was born and grew up in Buenos Aires, Argentina. An only child with imaginary friends, she spent a large part of her waking hours making up stories and working on mathematical equations. She has a Ph.D. in Physics from the University of Maryland and a Creative fiction writing certificate with honors from the University of California, Los Angeles. She has lived in Los Angeles since her twenties. She is currently completing two collection of poems and working on a series of personal essays. More details about her work, her publications and interests – she has too many and they tend to impact her efforts as a writer – can be found at www.mariacaponi.com/.

www.ingramcontent.com/pod-product-compliance
Lightning Source LLC
Chambersburg PA
CBHW072211150726

48002CB00005B/1759